Happy Birthday, 4/01

We look forward to spending time with you this summer!
J, B, L, H, + F

W9-CSX-236

South Carolina

THIRD EDITION

by

William Price Fox

The
Globe
Pequot
Press

Guilford, Connecticut

Cover and text design by Laura Augustine
Cover photo by Jim Schwabel/Index Stock
Maps created by Equator Graphics © The Globe Pequot Press
Illustrations by Carole Drong

Library of Congress Cataloging-in-Publication Data

Fox, William Price.
     South Carolina : off the beaten path / by William Price Fox. —3rd ed.
          p. cm. —(Off the beaten path series)
     Includes indexes.
     ISBN 0-7627-0833-6
     1. South Carolina—Guidebooks. I. Title. II. Series.

     F267.3 .F69 2001
     917.5704'44—dc21   00-049061

Manufactured in the United States of America
Third Edition/First Printing

To my brother Bob,
who sells the best Christmas trees
in Lexington County

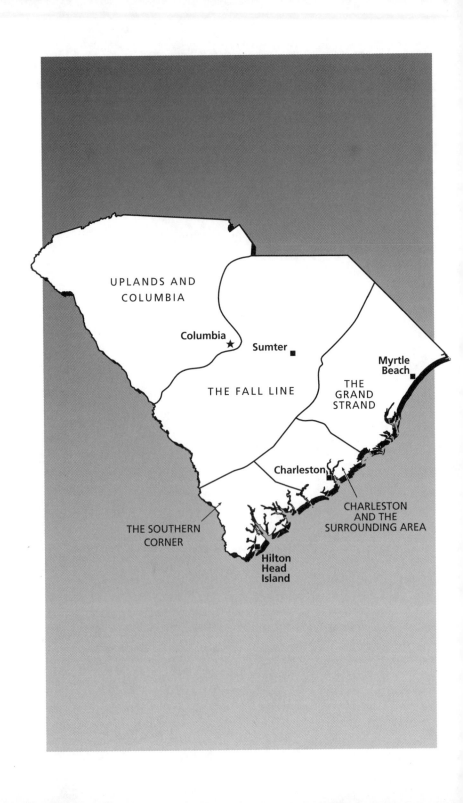

UPLANDS AND
COLUMBIA

Columbia ★   Sumter ■

Myrtle
Beach ■

THE FALL LINE   THE
GRAND
STRAND

Charleston ■

CHARLESTON
AND THE
SURROUNDING AREA

THE SOUTHERN
CORNER

Hilton
Head
Island

Contents

Help Us Keep This Guide Up to Date

Every effort has been made by the author and editors to make this guide as accurate and useful as possible. However, many things can change after a guide is published—establishments close, phone numbers change, hiking trails are rerouted, facilities come under new management, etc.

We would love to hear from you concerning your experiences with this guide and how you feel it could be made better and be kept up to date. While we may not be able to respond to all comments and suggestions, we'll take them to heart and we'll also make certain to share them with the author. Please send your comments and suggestions to the following address:

The Globe Pequot Press
Reader Response/Editorial Department
P.O. Box 480
Guilford, CT 06437

Or you may e-mail us at:
editorial@globe-pequot.com

Thanks for your input, and happy travels!

Introduction

My dad, who spent some time in Europe during World War II and who could hold the center of the room with the best of them, had his own theory about why South Carolina is so different from the rest of the country. When he was in Palermo, he said, he saw a painting of St. George slaying the dragon in which George was more than 6 feet tall and built like a wide receiver. The dragon came in at around 80 hands high, weighing more than fifty tons and throwing out a 60-foot sheet of blue-red flame. As he traveled north through Italy, Dad kept seeing the same painting, but while George stayed about the same size, the dragon kept losing weight and getting smaller. In Germany he was down to the size of a Clydesdale. Finally, in Copenhagen, Dad couldn't believe his eyes. "That dragon still looked like a dragon, but the artist had shrunk him down to the size of a good-sized rabbit. Old George was holding him up by one ear, and I mean he couldn't have dressed out no more than four pounds, tops."

Then he wrapped it up. "The way I see it, South Carolina is about like Palermo. We have more imagination down here, and you know, bigger visions. You get north, up above Richmond, and it's like Copenhagen."

Along with this rich imagination we also have the Gullah dialect, which is still heard down in the Low Country and out on the sea islands. Down here they still "read heads" and "work roots." They believe that "haint blue" and "haint green" painted on the door jambs and window trims will keep the evil spirits away and if you sweep your yard before the sun comes up, Doctor Death will keep on the other side of the road and go on about his business.

In Gullah, "he" stands for he, she, or it, and "um" stands for it, her, him or them. Many of the words and phrases run on pure sound and cadence, and with the high-low jackrabbit delivery much of it sounds like calypso. If it sounds good, it is good. Proper names can be name brands, road signs, or a quick and clever riff from a new tune. One woman near Beaufort, who was named during the Kennedy funeral, proudly displays Cathedral Rotunda Johnson above the red birds on her rural delivery mailbox. And over near Fripp Island, the town of Pocataligo is the compression of "poke a turtle's tail and he will go." Of the translatable Gullah proverbs and bromides, here are a fast few:

"Ef you play wid puppy, ee lick you face." (Familiarity breeds contempt.)

INTRODUCTION

"Ef you ent hab hoss to ride, ride cow." (Half a loaf is better than none.)

"Po buckra an dog walk one pat." (The poor man and the dog walk the same path.)

If South Carolina looks like anything, it's a slice of pie that has not only been badly cut but lifted out of the pan much too early. Starting in the northwest corner at the Chattooga River—about the spot where Sheriff James Dickey, the late poet-in-residence at the University of South Carolina, leaned on his patrol car in the film *Deliverance*—the South Carolina–North Carolina line runs east for 333 rugged miles to Little River and the Atlantic Ocean. From Little River the uninterrupted shoreline, with some of the best beaches in the country, stretches south over 200 miles to Tybee Sound, only a few miles from Savannah, Georgia. From here up the wide Savannah River back to the northwest corner and the Chattooga, it's 240 miles.

Roughly paralleling the South Carolina coastline and running across the center of the state is another line—the fall line. This separates two distinct regions—the Upcountry and the Low Country, with the sandy Midlands in between. Most of the Upcountry is plateaus with rolling hills, ragged woods, fast-moving streams, and red-clay earth. First settled by Germans, Scotch-Irish, and Welsh early in the eighteenth century, by 1800 the Upcountry had more than 30,000 small farmers who, with their self-sufficient way of life, had almost nothing in common with Low Country plantation owners. Today, while this region still has a great deal of farmland that produces soybeans, peaches, cotton, and tobacco, it is also a highly successful national and international manufacturing center. The plant most recently built here is the giant BMW plant in Greenville.

During the agricultural development of the Upcountry, the merchant-planters of the Low Country were living in the grand style of English gentlemen. Having named their first settlement Charles Town for England's King Charles II—the Merry Monarch who encouraged theater, horse racing, fine dining, dancing, and even golf—they were maintaining beautifully decorated town houses as well as sprawling and magnificent plantations and sending their children to London and Paris for their education.

On East Bay Street in Charleston, the oldest printers in the South, Walker, Evans and Cogswell, knowing the precarious ways of the American dollar, still hold onto their original Confederate money plates. Charlestonians are like this. They hold onto anything old: their houses, their furniture, their she-crab soup recipes, and their accents. It's this "holding-on" to the best aspects of the past and the sacred belief in landmarks that makes Charleston possibly the most beautiful city in the country. With its low skyline and lantern-lit cobblestone streets, you can stroll along at night with a good domestic wine and a little imagination and find yourself in southern France or Ireland's County Kerry, or, for the more literary, the pages of Jane Austen.

Charlestonians also, despite earthquakes, hurricanes, plagues, and outright ridicule, cling to their family names with a desperation that approaches that of the American Kennel Club. If a young married lady is introducing herself she might admit that she is now unfortunately a Hampton. "I'm Elizabeth Moultrie Hampton." Then, with a perfectly sensible "south of Broad Street" change of key, she'll quickly add, "wuzza Heyward," letting you know there were cotillions and better days in the not-too-distant past.

I grew up in the Midlands 100 miles north of Charleston in Columbia. Every day on the way to school I could see the green-domed capitol of the State House and the bronze stars on the western side marking the spots where Sherman's shells had struck. They are still there and will probably be there forever. We grew up here with history all around us. In the old section of town the streets are named for the Revolutionary generals Bull, Sumter, Pickens, and Marion. In the newer sections they bear the names of the Confederates: Lee, Jackson, Longstreet, Hampton, Pickett, and Green. In the section called "The Bottom," the names run the gamut from local politicians and famed prizefighters to attitudes and ambitions: Do Rite Alley, Easy Street, Sugar Ray Robinson Boulevard and Joe Louis Boulevard, and Captain Marvel Road (which is only 80 feet long and dead-ends into a trash pile). Everything else, from bridges and landfills to rest stops and runoff culverts, is named for Strom Thurmond.

In the small towns around Columbia, Greenville, and Spartanburg and on up to the North Carolina line, some traditions are set in stone and never change. The Atlantic Coast Line and the Southern tracks still gleam in the white gravel and the bright sun, and barefoot kids still walk the hot rails in the summertime. Fords, Chevys, and Plymouths, wrapped in honeysuckle and wisteria vines, still rust and rot out in the front yards and down in the drain ditches, and groups of three and four and five dogs still meet for all-night sessions under the streetlights at the crossroads.

We grew up here in the Midlands shooting squirrels in the swamp and carp in the river and rats at the trash pile. We sold iron to the iron man, paper to the paper man, and whiskey bottles to the bootleggers. We rode our bikes down the fifty or sixty or seventy steps of the State House, the courthouse, or whatever wedding-cake building was standing in the town square. We went to school here and joined the service here and came back from the service and went back to school here. Many of us left and went north or west or abroad, but almost all of us came back. Very few of us can put our finger on exactly why. Perhaps the best reason is that while we know it can get hot here in the summertime and pretty cool in the winter, the old Palmetto State is unlike any other place in the world.

Despite Hollywood's thigh-slapping, yee-hawing, chainsaw-dueling portrayal of South Carolinians, there is still a modicum of propriety and politeness down here not often found in the severe latitudes in the north. You will actually see men tip their hats to women and even give them their seats on the bus—there are no subways. And back in the smaller towns, suicides are toned down and usually reported as "after a short illness." But there are a few ground rules that you should know to make your trip here as easy and pleasant as possible.

Grits are served with all breakfasts. You can request home fries but don't be too surprised at what you get. Your best bet is to butter the grits, add pepper, mix them with your eggs, and not complain. An even better bet is to find a place that serves yellow grits instead of white—more on that later.

And contrary to what you've seen in the movies or read in the *National Enquirer*, there are no radar traps that track only northern license plates. The Highway Patrol officers are extremely helpful. If you have a flat tire or engine trouble just sit back and wait. They'll come along and make all the arrangements for towing, tire changing, and so on. As a matter of fact, most of the Highway Patrol's time is spent doing precisely this. Many of them are very good shade-tree mechanics.

In the Low Country be careful driving during a heavy rainstorm. Especially in downtown Charleston, often the rain will come with a high tide, and the streets will flood with a mix of fresh and salt water that can ruin your car in minutes. Do not try to drive through this. Sit still until the water recedes, or leave the car and come back for it later, when it dries out.

Due to the fact that South Carolina has been one of the poorest states for so many years, the federal government has stepped in and built an excellent highway system. The four interstates—I-20, I-77, I-26, and I-95—that crisscross the state may very well be the best and smoothest in the country. We also have well-equipped and beautifully maintained rest stops. And like most of the rest of the country, you can turn right on a red light.

Sunday blue laws are too complicated to discuss in detail. Basically they assume that we all should be in church on Sunday and have no business shopping, drinking, or browsing through the malls from 8:00 A.M. to noon. Each county has its own laws, but most of them are now allowing stores, movies, and malls to open after noon. While you cannot buy beer or wine on Sunday, bars that have paid a stiff Sunday sales tax can be open on Sunday nights until midnight. All this will vary from county to county. Another blue law, called the Sundown Law, stipulates that you can't buy whiskey from a package store after the sun goes down. This law is in effect every night of the week. You can, however, buy wine and beer from almost any store.

A very helpful resource is the Parks, Recreation and Tourism Board. Their phone number is (803) 734–0122 and they're open from 8:30 A.M. to 5:00 P.M. Monday through Friday. They can be contacted for free brochures and any and all information.

In South Carolina, everything happens on Labor Day. The football season opens, the Darlington 500 revs up, and across the sandhills and the Piedmont and on down the Congaree and the Cooper Rivers to Charleston, more than a hundred official barbecues, okra struts, catfish stomps, and demolition derbies all crank up at the same time. How to choose the best one is hard. But they're out there and all you have to do is check the papers or call the Chamber of Commerce.

Part of living in South Carolina and celebrating the survival of summer is the fall and the hundred fairs that crowd the calendars of the Chambers of Commerce. There are county fairs, town fairs, and fairs jimmied up at the crossroads with sawhorse tables for the pies and pickle relishes and rides that fold down from the backs of pickup trucks. The big one, the State Fair, is in Columbia in late September, and swirling around the centerpiece—a Saturn Rocket shipped up from Cape Canaveral—are more than 100,000 locals and not-so-locals eating elephant's ears, fried pies, and corn dogs, and then settling down to a first-class home-cooked meal in their favorite church tent while their kids ride everything from the Bumble Bee—for two-year-olds—to the Zipper, which after thirty years only the very young and the very drunk still ride.

South Carolina, with its own language, customs, and rhythms, is different. Very different. You'll see glimpses of it down on the coast in the shrimp boats and the oyster boats heading out at dawn and coming back in at dusk. You'll see it in the great blue heron as it glides across a marsh and settles under a moss-draped cypress tree, or in the possum—the small dog that doesn't bark—crossing a road carrying her litter. And

Exploding a Few South Carolina Myths

A hoop snake will not put its tail in its mouth and roll down a hill.

A diamond-backed rattler will not wrap around your leg to hold you still while it bites. Now that would be scary!

A red fox will not run on three legs (resting a fourth) when running from the dogs.

Fire ants will not swarm over your legs and then, on a mysterious signal from their leader, bite you all at once. But don't try this one out. They can be absolutely savage and terrifying and nothing short of a blowtorch can kill them.

you'll see it in that soft and sliding light at first dark that turns the roofs of Charleston from red to orange to gold to umber. I guess my Dad was probably right; if we're like anything, we're like Palermo because while we know that much of what we carry on about doesn't make a helluva lot of sense, we believe it anyway. In short, we have our own vision and version of history that works like this: it could have been, it should have been, it was. And in this happy delusion—sustained by azaleas in January and February, magnolias from March to August, gardenias, roses, wisteria, and 20-foot-high banana trees, fresh shrimp, and weather you can play golf in almost every day of the year—we still believe if Lee had had Jackson on his flank at Gettysburg, we could have won the day and the war, and the capital of these United States would be dead-center here between Greenville 100 miles north and Charleston 100 miles south, right here in Columbia where it was originally scheduled to be. We also believe what one of our leaders proclaimed years ago: that while South Carolina is too small for a good-sized plantation and too big for an insane asylum, it's the only state in the nation that doesn't envy Virginia.

H. L. Mencken, no slouch with superlatives, went one better when he called the South Carolina lifestyle "a civilization of manifold excellences, perhaps the best the Western Hemisphere has ever seen."

South Carolina Food Specialties

Pimento Cheese (Ruth's is the classic and can be found at most grocery stores.)

Boiled Peanuts (Buy raw peanuts, stick them in a TON of water, with a TON of salt, approximately four cups worth, and boil until they look as if they've lost all integrity!)

Pickled Boiled Eggs

Pecan Pie/Sweet Potato Pie

Pepper Jelly on cream cheese and crackers.

Pork Rinds (Can be bought in any store.)

South Carolina Facts

South Carolina was the eighth state to sign the Constitution and the first state to secede from the Union before the Civil War. Edisto Island, south of Charleston, decreed that if the state didn't secede, it would secede from South Carolina.

South Carolina grows more peaches than any other state, except California.

South Carolina has one of the oldest formal gardens in America—Middleton Gardens, finished in 1740.

South Carolina has 187 miles of coastline and arguably the best beaches in America. On some beaches you won't see a single soul for more than a mile, even in the middle of summer.

Kudzu on a hot day can grow more than a foot. Some teachers string it across the outside of a window so the pupils can actually watch it grow.

South Carolina State Symbols

State Tree—Palmetto Tree

State Nickname—The Palmetto State

State Animal—White-tailed Deer

State Game Bird—Wild Turkey

State Fish—Striped Bass

State Reptile—Loggerhead Turtle

State Insect—Praying Mantis

State Butterfly—Eastern Tiger Swallowtail

State Dog—Boykin Spaniel

State Bird—Carolina Wren

State Flower—Yellow Jessamine

State Motto—"Prepared in mind and resources. While I breathe, I hope."

Charleston and the Surrounding Area

Downtown Charleston

Charleston, which has been called The Holy City; The City by the Sea, Where the Ashley and the Cooper Rivers Meet to Form the Atlantic Ocean; and The Home of Rhett Butler, is the perfect place to begin a tour of the old Palmetto State. Settled in 1680, this remarkable town literally has to be seen to be believed.

My grandmother, who was from the midlands around Columbia, used to huff and hiss, "Charlestonians are all right but everybody knows they're just too poor to paint and too proud to whitewash."

You might consider seriously the recommendation that you don't even think about driving around Charleston. The streets are narrow, many are paved with cobblestones, and the one-way traffic can be a nightmare in rush hours. (Women wearing high heels will have a tough time negotiating cobblestones.) Parking on the street is almost impossible. The easier approach is to park your car in a downtown lot and forget it. The standard rate is about $5.00 a day.

Since Charleston and the Low Country area attract more than five

Hurricane Hugo

After Hugo whipped through Charleston in 1989, it left a number of stories behind that seem to increase and get bigger every year. One is of the farmer who tied six chickens to six posts, hoping they wouldn't get blown away. The idea worked and the chickens all lived to see another day—unfortunately the storm suction pulled out every single feather of every single bird. And the best line that's still around came from a mobile-home owner. "Man, when I looked outside in the morning there were refrigerators in the trees."

1

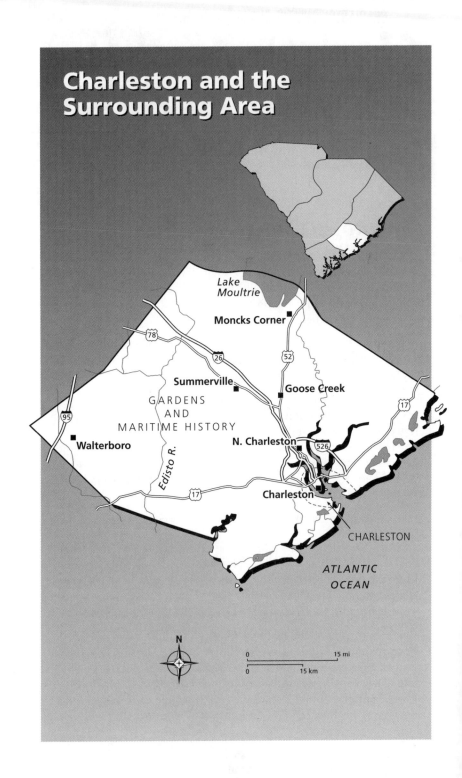

Charleston and the Surrounding Area

Lake Moultrie

Moncks Corner

78

26

52

Summerville

Goose Creek

17

GARDENS
AND
MARITIME HISTORY

95

Walterboro

N. Charleston

526

Edisto R.

17

Charleston

CHARLESTON

ATLANTIC
OCEAN

N

0   15 mi
0   15 km

CHARLESTON AND THE SURROUNDING AREA

AUTHOR'S FAVORITE PLACES

*Best Friend Bar at
The Mills House*

Dock Street Theatre

Tradd Street Press

The Calhoun Mansion

Angel Oak

Middleton Gardens

Boone Hall

The Battery Park

*St. Michael's
Episcopal Church*

Ocean Course at Kiawah

Charleston Country Club

million guests each year, hotel, guest house, and bed-and-breakfast owners have built a reputation for hospitality and extremely high standards. Charleston is famous for its bed-and-breakfasts in particular, and one local service does everything possible to match the guests to whatever sort of accommodations they want: Historic Charleston Bed and Breakfast (843–722–6606 or 800–743–3583).

Some bed-and-breakfasts provide bicycles that will help you get around the city on tours of your own arrangement. Lodgings in these homes and inns provide the wonderful feeling that you are staying in the very heart of the old city. Listed below are a few that are off the beaten path, yet have all the amenities for an enjoyable, comfortable stay.

Battery Carriage House at 20 South Battery, Charleston 29401. Rates range from $99 to $229. The rooms overlook the Battery and White Point Gardens and are furnished in period reproductions. Each room has its own private bath as well as separate air-conditioning and heating controls. Call (843) 727–3100.

The Kitchen House at 126 Tradd Street, Charleston 29401. Rates range from $100 to $120. The Kitchen House, built in 1732, is on one of the most beautiful blocks in the center of the Historic District, just yards from The Tradd Street Press and around the corner from the Four Corners of Law. It has free parking, complimentary breakfast, sherry, and wine. All rooms are air-conditioned, and all are beautiful. Call (843) 577–6362.

Loundes Grove Inn at 266 St. Margaret Street, Charleston 29403. Rates are $100. The inn is on the National Register of Historic Places and was built around 1786. It is the only plantation in the city on the Ashley River and has a spectacular view of the wide and winding river. As elegant as the facility is, it also has the modern touches of a pool, a whirlpool, and a river dock. Call (843) 723–3530.

Here's how you might begin a Charleston tour. Make ***The Mills House***—now a Holiday Inn—on the corner of Meeting and Queen your starting point in the very center of the old town and try a walking tour of a few spots close by. If you can, spend a night or two at The Mills. It's a beautiful restoration of what it was before the Civil War. As a matter of fact, on the second floor you can stand on the wrought-iron balcony where in 1861 Robert E. Lee stood and watched much of the old town burn.

The 215-room hotel is located at 115 Meeting Street and has accommodations that range from small rooms at $95 to suites at $250; parking is available at no extra charge. It has an outdoor swimming pool

The Mills House

on the third floor with a very comfortable sundeck where you can get a cool drink and a light snack. *The Best Friend Bar* on the lobby floor, with very good local musical talent, is the perfect spot after a night on the town. Across the beautiful marble lobby is *The Barbados Room,* which has earned the Mobil Travel Guide four-star award. Here they serve breakfast, lunch, and a romantic candlelit dinner for $19.95. Before you dine, be sure to sip a drink in the fountain courtyard. For reservations and information, call (843) 577–2400.

Still using The Mills House as a starting point, you can cross Meeting and walk exactly one block down Queen to Church to one of the oldest and most charming operating playhouses in the country, *The Dock Street Theatre.* The original theater, built in 1735, deteriorated after the Civil War and wasn't restored until 1935, when it was rebuilt by the WPA. During Spoleto, the annual music and art festival held in Charleston in late May and early June, the theater is the centerpiece for chamber music and plays. A few years back one of Tennessee Williams's last plays premiered here.

The Dock Street Theatre is open year-round for tours and individual browsing from 10:00 A.M. to 4:00 P.M. Monday through Friday unless a rehearsal is underway. The building, which has been reconstructed over and over again, dates back to 1736 and completely captures the Georgian architecture that flourished during that period. Dock Street seats 463 and has a pit and a parquet of thirteen boxes. Over the stage is a carved wood bas-relief of the Royal Arms of England. The cove ceiling has exceptional acoustic properties—when string quartets perform here during the Spoleto Festival any seat in the house is a good seat.

The old theater plays a leading role in the intellectual and cultural life of

TOP ANNUAL EVENT

Spoleto Music and Art Festival (last week in May, first week in June)

the city. All year long the theater features dramas, musicals, and family fare, as well as readings and recitals. Late May and early June are booked solid with concerts and plays during the Spoleto Festival. Call (843) 720–3968 for information.

A block and a half back up Queen and past The Mills House is *82 Queen,* a combination oyster bar, stand-up brass-railed pub, and fine restaurant. The building, formerly two adjoining nineteenth-century town houses, has a lovely courtyard dining area complete with awnings, umbrellas, and banks of shrubbery. Specialties here are seafood, beef, and fowl, with prices ranging from $12 to $25. The bar, which fronts on Queen, is a notorious hangout for local authorities on everything from ornithology to transcendentalism, and if you listen long enough you will probably hear it all. One local sage, deep in the grape, cornered me not too long ago with the red-hot, ice-cold information that Charleston inbreeding, which rivals that of the ancient Egyptians, has been going on so long and with such intensity that there isn't an empty attic on the whole peninsula.

A few doors back up Queen at number 72 is *Poogan's Porch,* which serves gumbos, jambalayas, and great crab cakes. The bread pudding and peanut butter pie are especially good and have become a tradition here on Queen. You can eat indoors or out on the veranda. For lunch, stay inside with the air-conditioning. For dinner, when it cools off, it's nice to eat outside. The name Poogan came from the dog who was left behind when the original owner sold the house and moved away. Since then the restaurant has changed hands several times, but each time the dog remained behind as the mascot until he died in 1979. Poogan's is open every day for lunch and dinner. Prices range from $15 to $22. Call (843) 577–2337.

From Poogan's Porch go back to The Mills House and follow Meeting Street south to Tradd Street. Turn left here and walk one block to *The Tradd Street Press and Book Store.* This is a stop you don't want to miss because this was the home of the painter Elizabeth O'Neill Verner (1883–1979), internationally famous for her pen-and-ink drawings and paintings of the Charleston skyline, its churches, and the local flower ladies and basket weavers. Prints of her work are here on exhibit and for sale along with a fine collection of cookbooks, guidebooks, and local ghost-story books from The Tradd Street Press. Many of the postcards and prints you'll see around Charleston are reproductions of drawings of this site by Elizabeth O'Neill Verner.

Directly behind Tradd Street Press at 91 Church Street, Charleston

29401, is *"Cabbage Row."* Originally four or five connected buildings around a central courtyard, today it is a boutique featuring designer clothing, gifts, jewelry, and a wide variety of accessories. It was here that "Porgy" of Dubose Heyward's book of that name lived. "Cabbage Row" was changed to "Catfish Row" for Dubose Heyward and George Gershwin's *Porgy and Bess.* In 1934 Gershwin moved to Charleston and lived a few miles away on Folly Beach where he and Heyward collaborated on the world-famous Charleston opera. Most of the staging was based on the courtyard, and much of Gershwin's inspiration for the score came from the sounds of the neighborhood (the strawberry man, the butter bean man, and the fresh shrimp man).

The Tradd Street Press and Book Store

Many of the letters of Gershwin to his brother Ira in New York describe life in Charleston in the 1930s and the devastation he witnessed from a hurricane. They also reveal a curious downside to the famous composer. Gershwin, hell-bent on self promotion, tried to get the Charlestonians to change Folly Beach to Gershwin Island. Fortunately Charlestonians knew where to draw the line and Folly Beach is still Folly Beach. These letters are available for reading in the main building of the Charleston Public Library at 404 King Street.

If you're a football, baseball, basketball, or golf fan and can't stand missing too much of the action, make a note of the *Charleston Sports Pub and Grill* at 41 South Market Street, Charleston 29401. A wide variety of sandwiches and beverages is available here. Prices are $4.00 to $7.00. Call (843) 853–2900.

On King Street about a block from The Mills House is one of the most elegant and tasteful women's clothing shops on the entire East Coast. Its name, *R.T.W.,* means ready-to-wear, and the place and the selections will make you ready to buy. Once you've tried something on and closed your eyes to the price, you'll probably want to wear it right then and there.

Jan McMenamin is the owner, and she has a marvelous eye for fashion and what particular women need to match their skin tone, eyes, hair and anything else that needs matching. As a matter of fact, she often goes abroad for a small group of her favorite customers and buys whatever she sees that she knows will please them. She is seldom, if ever, wrong. If you're in a quandary about what you should wear and how you should wear it, see her. For the nervous spouse fingering his/her credit card, Jan serves complimentary wine, brandy, coffee, tea, and an assortment of local sweets. You can park at the side of the store or one block away at the city parking lot right behind Mills House. Even if you don't buy anything, go in and look around—it's one of a kind.

Charleston Place, located at 205 Meeting Street, Charleston 20401, is one of the premier hotels in the South. Off the beautiful lobby is a small but fine selection of stores including Banana Republic, Polo, Laura Ashley, Gucci, and Doubleday Books. The lounge at the hotel is elegant, and while the piano players change frequently, they are all very, very good. Room rates begin at $189. Dinners range from $30 to $50. Call (843) 722–4900. It's not altogether "off the beaten path," but it's a place you should at least drop in at for a glass of something.

Hyman's Seafood at 215 Meeting Street, Charleston 29401, next to the Omni Hotel, has been voted the number one seafood restaurant in town. They serve fifteen to twenty-five different fish any way you like, as well as shellfish, aged beef, and several pasta dishes. Hyman's specializes in frying with olive oil, and their seafood can be had broiled, fried, or blackened. The okra soup is especially delicious and different.

Author's Note

*O*ne of the better walking-around stories down here about Charleston is about an elderly pair of sisters who had fallen on lean times. Despite their circumstances they insisted on telling everyone that nothing had changed and they were still summering in Paris. At night, when the rest of the town was asleep, they would slip out of their shuttered house and take their constitutional along the Battery. One night a child recognized them and wanted to say hello. Her mother held her back, saying, "No, dear, we don't speak to them in the summertime. They're still in Paris."

If this isn't the story that made Charleston "the most civilized town in the country," it certainly should be.

They're open seven days a week from 11:00 A.M. to 11:00 P.M. If you're driving, which you shouldn't be, park in the Omni Hotel garage next door. Call (843) 723–6000.

The Calhoun Mansion at 16 Meeting Street, Charleston 29401, is much more than a house, and a tour of this extravaganza is well worth the price of admission. To begin, it is 24,000 square feet (the average family home is approximately 3,000 square feet). Built in 1876, this Victorian showplace is divided into twenty-five rooms, each with different and elaborate tile floors and ornamental plaster molding. The ballroom, with its skylight and 45-foot-high ceiling, is the centerpiece. On the second floor is a great surprise for the children—a 14-foot stuffed and rampaging polar bear. One of the best-known movie-making secrets is the fact that the Calhoun Mansion was featured in the television miniseries *North and South* as the Pennsylvania home of the Hazzards. If you meet the right people at 82 Queen or The Best Friend at The Mills House, you might get a sunset tour of the roof of the old mansion, which may be the most beautiful view in all of Charleston. Open Wednesday through Sunday 10:00 A.M. to 4:00 P.M. Admission is $15.00 for adults and $7.00 for children ages six to ten; children under six are admitted free. Call (843) 722–8205.

After leaving the Calhoun Mansion, stroll up to the corner of Meeting and Broad, a junction known as *The Four Corners of Law.* Here, you'll see the flower ladies, whom Elizabeth O'Neill Verner so lovingly painted, selling roses, daffodils, or whatever is in season. Close by will be the basket ladies. If you're lucky, you'll hear them singing as they weave their ancient patterns from sweet grass, pine needles, and bulrushes and bind their elaborate work together with fiber strips from palmetto trees. The baskets, which come in a variety of shapes and sizes, are truly unique and can only be purchased here and out on Route 17 heading north. They last for years and make wonderful presents.

After this little excursion, which should give you a feeling for the old town, your next best stop is *The Charleston Visitor's Reception and Transportation Center* at 375 Meeting Street, Charleston 29403. One of the best visitor's centers in the country, it can save you time, money, and especially shoe leather if you decide to go on the walking tours. Its gracious and well-informed attendants can help you with almost everything, including tours, lodging, restaurants, parking, attractions, and entertainment.

Built in 1856, the Visitor's Center is a red-brick, high-ceilinged building that was formerly the Railroad Depot. Large-scale maps along with old photos and prints illustrate how the city has changed and developed since 1680, when the first settlers anchored here and came ashore. Computerized maps equipped with video stations are also available. You can call up information on interactive screens and request additional advice on direct-line telephones. A service counter with helpful attendants is at your disposal and is also a central location for obtaining tour and theater tickets.

A twenty-minute show entitled "Forever Charleston" is a combination of slides, music, city sounds, and narration by Charlestonians. Shown every half hour, it is a beautifully photographed production but seems long on charm and short on story, insight, and humor. It also needs a cleaner sound track. Nonetheless, buy a couple of pecan pralines from the attendant—they are delicious—and see it anyway. The tidewater panoramas and heron, egret, and alligator shots are worth the $2.50 admission and will get you in the perfect mood for touring the incredible homes, gardens, and plantations around the old city. The center is open from 8:30 A.M. to 5:30 P.M. daily but closes a half hour earlier in November, December, and February. It is also closed on Thanksgiving, Christmas, and New Year's Day. Call (843) 853–8000.

Boiled Peanuts

Look for and buy a sack of boiled peanuts, then see what happens. At first you will be repulsed by their appearance—they're brown and soft and look very, very suspicious. But get over it and try three or four. By the fourth or fifth, you will be hooked for life, and when you head back north you'll be loaded down with them. Unfortunately, like South Carolina peaches and sweet corn, they don't travel well and have to be shelled and eaten as close to the patch as you can get. You can buy them right on the street.

Next door to the Center you'll find a depot for the **Downtown Area Shuttles** (DASH), which leave every fifteen minutes for tours through different sections of Charleston. Tickets are 50 cents; a daylong pass is only $1.00. A good bet is to take several rides so you can figure out what area of town you'd like to explore by foot or horse-drawn carriage ride. Many people make the DASH depot their first stop, parking their cars here and taking a few quick rides in the shuttles before deciding where they would like to stay.

From the Visitor's Center, turn the corner to Jutson Street, and you'll find yourself at **The Bookstore Cafe,** at 412 King Street, Charleston 29403. The tables are small and the straight-back chairs are hard, but right here you can have one of the best breakfasts in town. A good dish before one of the long walking tours is the three-egg omelette served with bagels, cream cheese, and pancakes. Lunch is sandwiches, soup, and salads. They also serve cappuccino, café au lait, and espresso. Jammed in around the room are shelves of books, magazines, and newspapers, all of which are available for browsing or reading over a leisurely coffee. The food and coffee are excellent; prices are under $8.00. Open 9:00 A.M. to 2:30 P.M. Monday through Friday, and 8:00 A.M. to 2:00 P.M. Saturday and Sunday. Call (843) 720–8843.

From the Visitor's Center on Meeting Street, it's two blocks north to the *Gibbes Museum of Art* at 135 Meeting Street, Charleston 29401. Open Tuesday through Saturday from 10:00 A.M. to 5:00 P.M., Sunday from 1:00 to 5:00 P.M, closed Monday. Admission is $6.00 for adults, $5.00 for seniors and college students, $3.00 for children ages six to eighteen. Considered one of the best collections in the entire Southeast, this museum exhibits 500 eighteenth- and nineteenth-century portraits as well as sculpture and Japanese wood-block prints. The gift shop has a wonderful collection of note cards, postcards, and books that make excellent gifts. Don't be afraid to bring the kids here; there is plenty to keep them amused and busy. Call (843) 722–2706.

Right in the heart of Charleston at *Anything Marine* you can find just that, anything marine. Roscoe Anderson, the owner and operator, prides himself on being able to find anything you need for scuba diving, snorkeling, and fishing, as well as motorboat and sailboat equipment. If he doesn't have it he will get it for you. While he has some items that are new, most of his stock is secondhand and within the limits of almost any budget. Anderson also does a lively business buying and selling items on consignment and trading. Anything Marine is located at 487 Meeting Street, Charleston 29403; (843) 814–3651. Hours are 9:00 A.M. to 6:00 P.M. Monday through Saturday, closed Sundays. If you can't get to the store during regular hours, Roscoe will be glad to arrange an appointment for almost any other time.

Around the corner at 306 King Street, Charleston 29401, is *Sharky's Pizza,* which has probably the best pizza in town. They will deliver to your door from 4:30 P.M. till 2:00 A.M. This is an especially friendly and casual spot, and it's excellent for a late night snack. Beer and wine are served, and the help is superb. Call (843) 722–7200.

For the budget minded, only a few blocks away—we're still walking— you'll find *Jestine's Kitchen* at 251 Meeting Street, Charleston 29401. The specialties here are Low Country cooking, vegetables, fish, and a really wonderful fried chicken. The price range is from $3.00 to $15.00. Open from 11:00 A.M. to 9:30 P.M. Tuesday through Thursday, 11:00 A.M. to 10:00 P.M. Friday, 11:00 A.M. to 10:00 P.M. Saturday, 11:00 A.M. to 9:00 P.M. Sunday, closed Monday. Call (843) 722–7224.

Latasha's Taste of New Orleans, 43 Cannon, Charleston 29403, is a moderately priced excellent restaurant specializing in Cajun and Low Country cooking with wonderful rice dishes and desserts. Open for lunch Tuesday through Friday 11:00 A.M. to 3:00 P.M. and dinner Tuesday through Saturday 6:00 to 10:00 P.M. Closed Sunday and Monday. Beer and wine are served and the dinner prices range from $8.00 to $20.00. Excellent menu and service here. Don't be put off by the dark neighborhood, it's really quite safe and very friendly. Call (843) 723–3222.

Still walking, you can go to *S.N.O.B.* at 192 East Bay Street, Charleston, 29401, for exquisite dining and an equally exquisite atmosphere. The specialty here is Low Country cooking along with a number of very fine Continental dishes. One of the local favorites is shrimp and yellow grits. Prices range from $14 to $30 and wine is served. Lunch is served from 11:30 A.M. to 3:00 P.M., dinner from 5:30 to 10:00 P.M. While down south, try to get yellow grits rather than white. There's a big, big difference— the yellow is not overprocessed and has a much better taste. You can even buy it, although only in some stores. Call (843) 723–3424.

In the South Windemere Shopping Center, at 90 Folly Road, Charleston 29407, you'll find the *Med Deli.* Their specialties are pasta, seafood, sandwiches, and dinners, priced from $7.00 to $12.00, along with a huge wholesale arrangement for buying wine. The Med is open from 11:00 A.M. to 10:00 P.M. Monday through Saturday and serves lunch ($4.00 to $6.00) until 2:00 P.M. Closed Sunday. Call (843) 766–0323.

Vickerys, at 15 Beaufain, Charleston 29401, serves Cuban food and Low Country cuisine, as well as excellent seafood. This is a big and busy place and has a nice outdoor seating arrangement. Open daily, 11:30 A.M. to 1:00 A.M.. Price range here is $10 to $20. Wine is available. Call (843) 577–5300.

On up the street from The Mills House is the *Joseph Manigault House* at 350 Meeting Street, Charleston 29403. This classic example of the graceful Adam style was designed and built by the architect Gabriel Manigault in 1803. The unsupported circular staircase, which you will also see in the "Forever Charleston" show back at the Visitor's Center, is the centerpiece. In the 1920s the place was a broken-down boarding house, and for a while in the 1930s it was a service station. The dean of the Harvard School of Architecture and a number of Charlestonians took it upon themselves to help restore and furnish it with the period furniture you see here today. This is one of the few houses in Charleston that still has a gate house. Open 10:00 A.M. to 5:00 P.M. Monday through Saturday and 1:00 to 5:00 P.M. Sunday. Last tour is at 4:30 P.M. Admission is $8.00 for adults and $4.00 for children three to twelve. Call (843)

723–2926 or contact The Charleston Museum at (843) 722–2996 for combination tickets to all of the museum sites.

For one of the best views you simply have to visit the **Rooftop Terrace Bar** at **The Library At Vendue Inn,** located at 19 Venue Range, Charleston 29401. This popular spot offers a sweeping view of the harbor, the churches, and many of the copper roofs and chimneys of the old city. The cuisine here is distinctly southern, and everybody who comes here just keeps coming back. Full dinners cost around $30. Call (843) 577–7970 or (800) 845–7900. Open seven days a week from 5:00 to 11:00 P.M.

The **Nathaniel Russell House,** located at 51 Meeting Street, Charleston 29401, is another showcase home and a Charleston favorite. Spacious gardens surround this old house, recognized as one of America's finest examples of neoclassical architecture. Its elaborate plasterwork ornamentation, its free-flying staircase rising up through three complete stories without any visible means of support, and its beautiful proportions prompted the celebrated French aristocrat Henry DeasLesesne to proclaim it to be "beyond all comparison the finest establishment in Charleston." Open Monday through Saturday 10:00 A.M. to 5:00 P.M. and Sunday from 2:00 until 5:00 P.M. Admission is $5.00 for adults. Children under six are admitted free. Call (843) 722–3405.

Lodge Alley at 195 East Bay Street, Charleston 29401, is a place that anyone who has the slightest interest in renovation shouldn't miss. Ten years ago this was an ugly string of decaying warehouses. Today it is a beautiful inn with a fountain at center court and an excellent restaurant. The specialties at the restaurant are roast squab and rack of lamb, as well as seafood and Low Country cuisine. If you don't stay here or eat here, at least stop by for a drink at the small, intimate bar overlooking the courtyard. Call (843) 722–1611.

Gaulart and Maliclet at 98 Broad Street, Charleston 29401, in the heart of the city, prides itself on being fast and French. They are just that—and given the high quality of their food and fine service, surprisingly economical. I had a cup of delicious split-pea soup, a sandwich of paté and blue cheese, and excellent coffee for around $6.00. They have a very fine wine list but best of all, their steady customers all seem remarkably upbeat and happy and seem to know one another. This is one of the smaller but really very fine Charleston surprises. It's a great place to drop in for lunch or dinner and sit at the bar and listen to the music and the local gossip. Open 8:30 A.M. to 4:00 P.M. Monday, 8:30 A.M. to 10:00 P.M. Tuesday–Thursday, and 8:30 A.M. to

10:30 P.M. Friday and Saturday. Call (843) 577–9797.

Put this one on the very top of your list: ***Robert's of Charleston Dinner Restaurant*** at 182 East Bay Street, Charleston 29401. Call (843) 577–7565 or (800) 977–7565. Save up a few bucks, shore up your appetite, and take the little woman or man here. It will be the best money you've spent in a long, long time. Billed as "Charleston's most romantic restaurant," it's far more than that. The centerpiece is one of the most extraordinary characters on the penninsula, Robert Dickson. Not only is he the remarkable host of one of the best restaurants on the *entire coast* but he's also a wonderful singer, from Puccini to German Leider to every song you can remember from Broadway shows. Every few years he takes a group of very lucky Charlestonians to Italy, where they visit the great eating establishments and Robert takes requests and sings to them before, during, and after the meals. I have a close friend who went with him the last time and plans to go again and again for the rest of his life. Recently, Robert Dickson pulled off an event we'll be talking about forever. He invited two full Tuscany choirs—a grand total of thirty-one people—to entertain the lucky diners at the restaurants. The two choirs had already given performances at St. Michael's Church and Alumni Hall at the University of Charleston. At Robert's Restaurant they divided up into four groups and sang secular Renaissance music *a cappella*. The performance was spellbinding and will long be remembered here in the old "City by the Sea." So stop by, meet Robert Dickson, and at least have a glass of wine. There's no telling what he will be up to next. Prices at Robert's start at $25.

Gardens and Maritime History

Not only is there a lot to see and do in Charleston, there is a great deal just outside the city limits on the barrier islands—namely, Isle of Palms, Sullivan's Island, Seabrook, and Kiawah. South of Charleston on Route 17—The Savannah Highway—you'll see the sign for Seabrook and Kiawah Islands. Turn here on Bohicket Road and proceed exactly 7.3 miles to the sign for ***Angel Oak*** and turn right. The sandy road will look deserted (because it is) and you'll think you're on the wrong road. But stay with it for about a half mile and you'll see a sight you will never, ever forget—the Angel Oak. It's one of the true American wonders. Don't forget your camera for this one.

While you are here, squint your eyes and in a certain slant of light you can easily imagine dinosaurs scratching their backs on the big limbs while leather-winged pterodactyls perch on top scratching their fleas and watching the salt marsh for their next meal. A few Angel Oak specifics: height 65 feet; circumference 25.5 feet; area of shade 17,000 square feet; largest limb circumference 11.25 feet; length 89 feet. In other words, it has to be seen to be believed.

In the opposite direction, 14 miles northwest of Charleston on Route 61, is the site of America's oldest landscaped garden, at *Middleton Place,* 4300 Ashley River Road, Charleston 29414. The plantation was laid out on the banks of the Ashley River, and the grounds include an authentic plantation house, a modern inn, and one of the world's most beautiful gardens.

A recent addition at Middleton is an actual freedman's dwelling furnished as it was in the 1870s when it was lived in by freed slaves who stayed on the plantation after the Emancipation. You will also see blacksmiths, potters, weavers, and carpenters who will explain and demonstrate what they are doing and tell you about the plantation's history. The main house was built in 1741 but was burned by Union troops in 1865. As the story goes, the soldiers drank wine and had a glorious dinner with heavy silver and fancy linen at the main house, then they set fire to it and left.

Perhaps the best part of Middleton Place is the incredible view from the high terraces of the azalea, camellia, and rose gardens that roll down the hill into the Butterfly Lakes. The restaurant here serves Low Country dishes for lunch and dinner on Friday and Saturday only. The gift shop sells plantation-crafted wares. During the Spoleto Festival, Middleton often serves as the site for the grand finale. With the Charleston Symphony Orchestra playing from the water's edge against a backdrop of fireworks, the huge crowd sits on blankets on the gently rolling terraces that were laid out here in 1741. Open daily from 9:00 A.M. to 5:00 P.M. Call (843) 556–6020.

For the sheer beauty of it, plus wonderful food, you simply can't beat dining at the *Middleton Place Restaurant,* at 43 Ashley River Road, Charleston 29414. Call (843) 556–6020 or (800) 782–3608. This popular spot overlooks America's oldest landscaped gardens and serves plantation fare for lunch from 11:00 A.M. to 3:00 P.M. and elegant, candelit dinners every evening from 6:00 to 9:00 P.M. Specialties include she-crab soup, panned quail, venison, and many more. Prices range from $5.00 to $20.00. Closed Sundays. Call (843) 722–2628 or (800) 789–3678.

Continuing on Route 61, turn right at Route 165 and in a few miles you'll come to **Summerville,** one of the most charming towns in the South. Formerly a winter resort for Charlestonians and Columbians, its streets ramble in curves through the trees. The lavish bloom of azaleas, camellias, and wisteria glow against the dark background of pines. Small boys still rush out to your car if they suspect you're a tourist, holding up signs marked "Guide." Only two blocks from the business section is the Azalea Park and Bird Sanctuary. More than 800 specimens of native plants grow in the park. In the winter thousands of migratory birds stop here on their way south. This is a delightful town, and you will see not only enormous areas covered with azalea and camellias but also hedges and ornamental shrubs of tea plants. Back in 1890 Dr. Charles U. Shepard began experimentation in commercial tea growing and for a short time Lipton Tea helped finance his enterprise. Although his farm eventually failed, the knowledge of planting tea lived on and can be seen all over Summerville in the hedges and ornamental shrubs. Incidentally, the tea plant is a close cousin of the camellia.

Heading back toward Charleston on Route 61, about 5 miles after passing Middleton Place again, you will see Drayton Hall, also known as **Magnolia Gardens,** at 3550 Ashley River Road, Charlston 29414. Call (843) 571–1266. The 300-year-old plantation is the ancestral home of South Carolina's illustrious Drayton family; ten generations have used it since 1670. Internationally famous, it is considered to be one of America's oldest man-made attractions. Noted for its springtime beauty, it features more than 250 varieties of azalea and 900 varieties of camellia, as well as beautiful seasonal blooms every month of the year.

This is an ideal place for the kids. You can paddle a canoe through the waterways of the 125-acre waterfowl refuge or view it from a wildlife observation tower along its walkways. Children will also enjoy Magnolia's rare mini-horses, as well as its petting zoo where the kids can feed and pet a score of animals. Even your pets are welcome here—as long as they stay on a leash. The newest addition at Magnolia in the wildlife preserve is The Audubon Swamp Garden, which is sixty acres of black water in a cypress and tupelo swamp. The garden is accessible via boardwalks and dikes and is home to every species of Low Country wildlife. To reach Magnolia Gardens from Charleston drive 10 miles west on Route 61. You'll see the signs. Magnolia Gardens is open 8:00 A.M. to 5:30 P.M. every day. Admission is $11.00 for adults, $8.00 for teenagers, $5.00 for children ages six to twelve, and free for children under age six. Call (843) 571–1266.

Birds of Prey

I f you see a hawk, eagle, owl, vulture, falcon, kite, or osprey—any raptor bird—on the side of the road that has been hit by a car and is in trouble, *there is something you can do about it.* Wrap the bird up in a towel and place it in a dark box or trunk if it's not too hot. You must keep it out of the light. Then call the **South Carolina Center for Birds of Prey** at (843) 928–3494. They will arrange for you to drop it off at a convenient place where their staff, or one of their countless volunteers, will pick it up and take it to their headquarters on Route 17 north of Charleston. As a matter of fact, if you are in some state other than South Carolina you can still call the number and they will give you the number of the nearest Birds of Prey Recovery Hospital.

The Center, founded by Jim Singleton of Charleston, is a modern, well-equipped hospital owned and supported by tax-free contributions only and is probably one of the finest and best-managed in the entire Southeast. When they receive an injured bird they quickly x-ray it to find out the damage, then they set the bones, treat it, and place it in a holding area where in most cases it recovers. Every year they treat and release more than 200 raptor birds.

Recently they reset a bald eagle's wing and kept him in their holding building for weeks to make sure the wing had healed properly. I was there when they released it, and I'm here to say it was a sight to see. First of all, the bird had a wingspan of 5 to 6 feet, and when it took off you could see the pine straw and the leaves on the ground move and you could feel the breeze. He flew to a pine tree limb about a hundred yards away, took a long look around to get his bearings, said his good-byes, and headed out for Colorado—where he was probably from. For smaller birds that are injured, I guess the best bet is the Audubon

Facts about Raptor Birds

A hawk, if it could read, could read the New York Times *from a mile away. It can also kill a full-sized crow by merely squeezing it with its talons.*

An owl can swivel its head 270 degrees.

An osprey, if it sees that you can see into its nest, will build it higher. It is the only raptor that does not have a subspecies. In other words, it's the perfect bird and has needed no changes.

An osprey carries fish with the head forward and the tail behind to limit drag.

Society. Oh, and what happens to birds that recover and still can't fly away? These birds are given a happy home right here and are used in educational projects throughout the state.

In the general area of Magnolia Gardens and Middleton Place on Highway 171, between I–26 and Route 17, you will find **Charles Towne Landing.** This is the site of the first permanent English settlement in the state and the birthplace of South Carolina. Today it's preserved as a national treasure—a one-of-a-kind state park filled with history and natural splendor. The Landing is also a great place for children. Here they can climb aboard the *Adventure,* a full-scale replica of a seventeenth-century trading vessel, and see the settlement's original fortified town from the water. They can explore eighty acres of lush gardens or walk through the winding trails of the natural habitat zoo, which features wolves, puma, bears, and bison. A hands-on activities exhibit for the kids uses household tools and crafts common in the seventeenth century. For further information contact Charles Towne Landing, 1500 Old Town Road, Charleston 29407 or call (843) 852–4200.

If you're still in a visiting-a-garden mood after you've visited Magnolia Gardens, you're only 12 miles from **Cypress Gardens,** a 162-acre swamp garden created in the 1920s and festooned with flower-lined pathways. Each spring a profusion of azaleas, dogwood, daffodils, and wisteria are reflected in the mirrors of the black waters. Outdoor enthusiasts and bird-watchers will particularly enjoy the two rambling nature trails here, which wind through habitats and nesting areas for the alligator, pileated woodpecker, river otter, barred owl, and wood duck. You can explore the gardens in the traditional manner, with a guided flat-bottomed boat tour, or you can rent a canoe and paddle yourself off the beaten trail to who knows where.

From Charleston take I–26 to exit 208 (Moncks Corner). Follow Highway 52 north a couple of miles and watch for signs to Cypress Gardens. Open February through December. Admission for adults is $7.00, seniors pay $6.00, children six through twelve pay $2.00, and children under six are admitted free. Call (843) 553–0515.

And finally, one more plantation! **Boone Hall** is the one everyone wants to see—the plantation that inspired the plantation Tara from *Gone with the Wind.* The entrance alone, through two magnificent columns of eighty-eight live oaks, is worth the price of admission. Captain Thomas Boone planted one hundred live oaks in 1743, and, amazingly enough, eighty-eight have survived. Visitors can tour the renovated Greek Revival–style mansion and walk through the azalea and camellia gardens. Nine original slave cabins are also here. Boone Hall is 8 miles north of Charleston on Route 17 at 1235 Long Point Road, Mount Pleasant 29464. Admission is $12.50 for adults, $10.00 for senior citizens, and $6.00 for children ages six through twelve. Children under six are admitted free. Open all year. April through Labor Day, hours are 8:30 A.M. to 6:30 P.M. daily except Sunday, when hours are 1:00 P.M.–5:00 P.M. Open the rest of the year from 9:00 A.M. to 5:00 P.M. daily, except Sunday, when hours are 1:00–4:00 P.M. Call (843) 884–4371.

Crossing over the Cooper River Bridge you'll find the popular **Shem Creek Bar and Grill** at 508 Mill Street, Mount Pleasant 29464, where they pride themselves on "cookin' on the Creek." This is the home of Sloppy John's Oyster Bar and Dock. Shem's is also accessible by water, and boats park right at the bar. They specialize in grilled seafood and beef, served indoors or outdoors on the "gazebos" overlooking Shem Creek. The place is big and at times noisy, but it has a wonderful, salty ambiance, fine food, and an excellent staff. The kids will like the mounted river otter on display right across from the cashier. Lunches from $6.00 to $12.00. Dinner from $12 to $27. Open year-round. Call (843) 884–8102.

Patriot's Point Naval and Maritime Museum is in Charleston Harbor and is one of the most unusual and best-run museums in the country. Call (843) 884–2727. A mile from the Cooper River Bridge are four permanently moored ships, twenty aircraft, and the World War II aircraft carrier *Yorktown.* You will find the destroyer *Laffey,* the Coast Guard cutter *Ingham,* the submarine *Clamagore,* and the nuclear-powered ship *Savannah,* which can be boarded, inspected, and photographed at your convenience. Again, be sure to pack your camera and take along plenty of color film.

To give you some idea of the size and weight of the *Yorktown,* consider this: During Hurricane Hugo, which practically lifted Charleston up and set it back down again, the carrier barely moved. The ship served in combat at Truk, the Marianas, Iwo Jima, and Okinawa in World War II. Later it picked up the crew of *Apollo VIII,* the first manned spacecraft to circle the moon.

The hangar and flight decks of the carrier are now set up as a journey through the history of naval aviation. Here you'll see many of the prop-driven fighters, bombers, and torpedo planes that fought throughout the Pacific. You'll see a B-25 bomber similar to the ones of General Jimmy Dolittle's famous "Sixty Seconds Over Tokyo" raid. You'll see fighters that provided the air support during the Korean War. A great collection of some of the world's most feared jets are displayed here along with distinguished battle histories spanning from Korea to Desert Storm. You'll see the actual living quarters of the pilots and the "ready rooms" where they were briefed on their upcoming missions.

While aboard the carrier, you'll also want to stop by the ship's theater for a complimentary viewing of the Academy Award–winning film *The Fighting Lady,* which features some of the most incredible World War II dogfight footage ever taken.

The centerpieces on board the *Yorktown* are the twenty vintage aircraft ranging from a World War II basic trainer to the jets that ruled the skies of the Korean, Vietnam, and Persian Gulf wars. They even have a World War II torpedo bomber much like the one former President George Bush pancaked in the Pacific.

The museum is open daily from April 1 through September 30 from 9:00 A.M. to 7:30 P.M. From October 1 through March 31 hours are 9:00 A.M. to 6:30 P.M. Admission is $11.00 for adults, $5.00 for children ages six through eleven, free for children under six. Call (843) 884–2727.

If you're staying overnight in Charleston the **Spiritline Dinner Cruise** is one of the musts on your list. Get on board the *Spirit of Carolina,* which leaves from Patriots Point in Mount Pleasant for a three-hour evening of dinner, live entertainment, and the best possible view of the old city at dark. It's a beautiful trip and one you won't soon forget. The food, entertainment, and service are excellent. It gets cool out in the harbor, so take along a sweater.

Spiritline also offers $1\frac{1}{2}$-hour sightseeing trip in the daytime and a $2\frac{1}{4}$-hour trip out to the Fort Sumter National Monument and Museum. Call for information at (843) 722–2628 or (800) 789–3678.

Price for the dinner cruise Sundays–Thursdays is $37.85 per person. On Friday and Saturday, it's $40.85.

Prices for the Harbor Tour are $10.50 per person, $5.50 for children ages six to eleven, and free for children under five.

Prices for Fort Sumter Tour are adults $11.00, children ages six to eleven $6.00, and children under six free.

There are a number of great places to eat outside Charleston, including **Slightly Up the Creek,** at 130 Mill Street, Mount Pleasant 29464, which offers excellent waterfront dining on great Low Country cuisine in the old village at an affordable price. Because it is a very popular place frequented by the locals, it would be wise to call (843) 884–5005 for reservations. If the phone is busy just go on out. Lunch is served Monday–Friday 11:30–3:00 P.M.; dinner is every night from 5:30, Saturday from 5:00–10:00 P.M. Prices range from $8.00 to $20.00.

Village Diner, at 1275 Ben Sawyer Drive, Mount Pleasant 29464, is one of those unforgettable places where breakfast is served all day, every day. They are also open on Sundays. Hours are 8:00 A.M. to 8:00 P.M. Monday–Saturday; 8:00 A.M. to 8:00 P.M. on Sunday. One of their specialities is homemade biscuits that *really* taste homemade. They also do a great job on crisp fried bacon, which will stand up if you lean it against another slice. Prices are not only in the ballpark, they are amazing. Breakfast, lunch, and dinner are all right around $6.00. Buffet is slightly higher with a different, delicious specialty every day. Call (843) 881–9292.

Momma Brown's at 1471 Ben Sawyer Road, Mount Pleasant 29464, is hard, hard, hard to beat. In the Carolina sweepstakes on barbecue they're way out in front of the pack; no one else is even close. They specialize in the great vinegar- and pepper-based sauce that is famous down here in the Low Country. Open Tuesday through Saturday from 11:00 A.M. to 9:00 P.M. and Sunday from 11:00 A.M. to 3:00 P.M., closed Mondays. Prices vary from $6.50 to $8.00. Call (843) 849–8802.

Another wonderful place, especially for eating South Carolina seafood, is *Bowen's Island* at 1870 Bowen's Island Road, Mount Pleasant 29412. This restaurant is as rustic and back-roads as it can get. As a matter of fact, unless you're ready for it you'll take one look, hit reverse, and back right on out. But stick with it. First off, you have to find it. The best bet is to stop in the Folly Beach area and ask anyone. Everyone goes here and has been going here forever. Once you get over the shock of seeing it, you'll love it. Everything is fresh because for years the Bowens have been running the whole show—from procuring the seafood to cleaning it to getting it on the table. The dress code is ultra-casual, which means jeans are the top of the line. Inside the concrete-block house, which looks like a cell block, you'll see the old walls are covered with names and one-liners that go back to the 1940s. Check the spiral notebooks written in by generations of Bowen diners and be sure to add your name and comments. Get here early and tour the holding tanks for the crabs and find out why Folly Beach oysters are the best on the coast. If you have any questions about crabs, oysters, clams, and seafood in general (such as how to tell when it's fresh or questionable or really off-limits), this is the place to find out the answers. The specialties here are

Fried Oysters

It might not be on the menu but you can ask for it and probably get it . . . fried oysters and yellow grits.

fried shrimp, crab cakes, and all-you-can-eat oysters at prices you can't beat. Once again, don't be put off by the outside appearance; inside, once the food is served and the ancient jukebox is on, it's terrific. Open only Monday through Saturday from 5:00 to 10:00 P.M. Prices range from $10 to $15 tops. No credit cards. Call (843) 795–2757.

At 819 Coleman Boulevard, Mount Pleasant 29464, *J. Bistro* specializes in Nouveau American, with a price range of $15 to $40 for dinner. Open Tuesday through Sunday 5:00 to 10:00 P.M. They also serve an excellent brunch on Sunday, from 10:30 A.M. to 2:30 P.M. Call (843) 971–7778.

Atlanticville Restaurant and Cafe, at 2063 Middle Street, Sullivan's Island 29482, is located in a traditional island beach house, where you can sit on the patio before or after dinner and watch the sun set. Inside, the atmosphere is casual but the food is elegant, and there is an extensive wine list. One of the features here is "Thai Tuesday," which is very popular with the natives. Call (843) 883–9452. Open daily from 5:30 to 10:00 P.M. Sunday brunch from 10:00 A.M. to 2:30 P.M. Prices range from $5.00 to $10.00 for lunch, and $25 to $35 for dinner.

Of course, no visit to Charleston would be complete without a trip to *The Battery.* But first a little background on the site. This tip of the Charleston peninsula was first called White Point Garden due to the

white expanse of sand and the bleached oyster shells that identified it as a prominent marker when the colonists were settling here in 1670. The point later gained fame in 1718 when Stede Bonnet and forty of his fellow pirates "took the air" here with ropes around their necks, an event that brought an end to the coastal piracy that had plagued the nearby waters previously.

The Battery

On April 12, 1861, Charlestonians sought vantage points here to watch the Confederate guns fire on the Union troops stationed at Fort Sumter. The cheers went up, Rhett Butler groaned (fictionally, years later in

Margaret Mitchell's *Gone with the Wind*), and the Civil War had started. When Union forces left Fort Sumter, the Confederates occupied it, digging in for the next two years under heavy bombardment and keeping the Union from taking Charleston.

In June of 1863 Union troops gained control of Folly Island and the mouth of the Stono River. On July 10 they crossed Lighthouse Inlet to the southern end of Morris Island and by nightfall had secured half of the island and were within artillery range of Fort Sumter, which by then had become a symbol of Confederate resistance. Defending the tip of Morris Island and Charleston at the place formerly known as White Point Garden was the Confederate Battery Wagner.

On July 18, the Union forces advanced up the beach. It was this battle that was depicted in the film *Glory,* starring Morgan Freeman, Matthew Broderick, and Denzel Washington. Spearheading the attack was the 54th Massachusetts Regiment under the leadership of Colonel Robert G. Shaw, the twenty-five-year-old son of a wealthy Boston abolitionist. The bloody battle saw more than 40 percent of the black troops killed; Colonel Shaw died with them.

The courage of the 54th proved once and for all to the leaders of the North and the South that black soldiers could fight. By 1865, a total of 178,895 black soldiers had enlisted in the Union Army—more than 12 percent of the North's fighting force. Recent southern historical work has shown that black soldiers also fought with the Confederacy.

By September the Union controlled all of Morris Island, only 1,300 yards of water away from Fort Sumter. For almost two more years the Confederates held out under more heavy bombardment. Finally in February of 1865 they withdrew in the night when they knew Charleston city was falling to Sherman.

Today The Battery, filled with war memorials, cannons, and a monument on the spot where the pirate Stede Bonnet was hanged, is one of the most pleasant parks in the city and is the ideal place for turning the kids loose. You might follow the custom of hundreds of old Charlestonians who believe that no evening is complete without watching the sun set from here and then lighting up a cigar and taking a luxurious stroll along the ancient seawall.

Back in downtown Charleston at the Visitor's Center at 360 Meeting Street, Charleston 29403, you'll be across the street from **The Charleston Museum.** Call (843) 722–2996. This is the first and oldest museum in the country, founded in 1773. Some exhibits focus on the

Native Americans who were here first, others on the Revolutionary War or the Civil War; another celebrates the birth of "The Charleston Dance."

Children will especially enjoy the "Discover Me" room with amazing interactive exhibits. Toys, games, clothes, and even children's furniture have been collected from the past for entertainment and education. For a full grasp of old Charleston's culture and contributions to the country and to the world, no trip would be complete without a visit here. Call (843) 722–2996.

Charleston has long prided itself on religious tolerance, evidenced by the fact that here you can find the oldest Baptist, Catholic, and Jewish houses of worship in the country.

The oldest of these is the *First Baptist Church* at 61 Church Street, Charleston 29401. Founded in 1682, the church was redesigned in 1820 by Robert Mills, the first American-born architect and the designer of the Washington Monument. This structure is one of the earliest Greek Revival buildings in the nation. Morning services and Sunday school are held here on Sunday; a vesper service is held on Sunday evening. Wednesday is Family Night, with supper and a prayer service. A concert series here features organ recitals and chamber music programs. Call (843) 722–3896.

In 1789 *St. Mary's Church* was established at 89 Hasell Street, Charleston 29401. This is the oldest Roman Catholic church in South Carolina and is famous for its stained-glass windows, oil paintings, and graveyard. Call (843) 722–7696.

Kahal Kadosh Beth Elohim, at 90 Hasell Street, Charleston 29401, was founded in 1749 and is the oldest synagogue in continuous use in the United States. According to synagogue records it is the oldest surviving Reform synagogue in the world. Services are held Friday evenings and Saturday mornings. Call (843) 723–1090.

St. Michael's Episcopal Church, on the corner of Meeting and Broad Streets near the Four Corners of Law at 14 St. Michael's Alley, Charleston 29401, was established in 1761. The simple and elegant structure with a walled graveyard has long been a landmark and can be seen in many of the paintings and photographs of the old city. Call (843) 723–0603.

Another beautiful church is *St. Philip's Episcopal,* 146 Church Street, Charleston 29401, on the corner of Church and Queen Streets. Both of these churches have been lovingly sketched and painted by Elizabeth

Golf Courses

(See page 5).

While Charleston and the Low Country are only 5 to 10 feet above sea level, the land rises to 3,560 feet 200 miles away at Sassafras Mountain, west of Greenville. This elevation difference, along with the great varieties of trees and soil, account for the fact that South Carolina is considered by many to be the best state in the country for its variety of great golf courses.

O'Neill Verner; prints of these sketches are modestly priced and are available at the Tradd Street Press. (See page 5).

Emanuel African Methodist Episcopal Church at 110 Calhoun Street was established in 1818. Its present building has been in use since 1891. With its congregation of more than 1,600 members, the church is very active in assisting the Charleston Interfaith Crisis Ministry as well as a score of charitable organizations. Two Sunday morning worship services are held here. A Thursday evening service and a Bible study group on Monday are also offered. Call (843) 722–2561.

A few years back I wrote a book entitled *Golfing in the Carolinas.* The assignment was simply to pick out the fifty courses in the Carolinas I liked best, play each of them, write a few words, and then go on to the next one. I learned a great deal on my tour, especially about master architects Donald Ross, Alister McKenzie, Robert Trent Jones, Tom Fazio, and Pete Dye, whom I watched build the **Ocean Course** on Kiawah Island. This course, which hosted the 1991 Ryder Cup matches, is an absolute must for any golfer with a set of sticks. Incidentally, you go right by the Angel Oak on your way here (see page 13).

Ten of the Ocean Course holes run right along the ocean. Considering the cost of oceanfront lots on Kiawah, the course may very well be one of the most expensive ever built. It is certainly the hardest to play. When the wind is up, which is almost every afternoon, very few golfers break 90. During the '91 Ryder Cup matches, pros were actually aiming into the gallery hoping to avoid the howling wind, and the pro Mark Calavecchia was reduced to actual tears—he had to withdraw from the final holes. While windblown and terrifying, the Ocean Course is a course all golfers should play just to be able to say they tried it. Fortunately it's semiprivate, and a simple phone call to (843) 768–7272 can get you a tee time. Try to come early to avoid the afternoon wind, and bring plenty of balls.

While South Carolina doesn't have such venerable courses as Shinnecock out on Long Island, New York, or Brookline near Boston, it has something else—incredible golf weather. When you consider that northern courses are closed down four and five months a year and that down here in the so-called "hard lard belt" we play almost every day, the rest of the golfing country simply pales by comparison. South Carolina also has a wonderful variety of courses, ranging from the 4,000-foot mountain courses to the sandhills to the Low Country and the ocean. While most northern courses are private, most of South Carolina's are semiprivate, which means a great number of golfers will have the opportunity to play on a wide variety of great courses. A few of the better ones include Tom Fazio's famous **Wild Dunes** on The Isle of Palms (843–886–9704), Jack Nicklaus's **Turtle Point** on Kiawah (843–768–7272), Arthur Hill's **Dunes West** in Mount Pleasant (843–856–9000), and Pete Dye's aforementioned Ocean Course.

Because Charleston offers so much to the visiting tourist it may very well be the ideal city for the "golf widow" and the ever-growing number of "golf widowers." Cases are on file of golfers who arrive here determined to play four or five of the dozen famous courses around town but who, after looking at the calendar of events, the long list of great restaurants, and the sights to be seen, wind up not getting a single club out of their bags. But for the golfer who has to play, this is the place to do it. The truly spectacular courses here, which year in and year out make the list of the top fifty in the country, are the Ocean Course and Wild Dunes.

For the golf historian, a trip out to the private **Charleston Country Club** should be fascinating. Despite the records showing that the first course in America was open for play in 1898 at St. Andrews in Yonkers, New York, the game was being played here almost 250 years earlier under the encouragement of King Charles II. King Charles was an avid golfer, and a 1698 print shows him being interrupted in the middle of a round to read news of an Irish rebellion. At the club you can see the old menus from the late seventeenth century and golf notices from the early eighteenth. The retired professional here is the internationally famous Henry Picard, and one of his protégés is the professional Beth Daniels. For information, call the club secretary at (843) 795-0422.

PLACES TO STAY IN CHARLESTON AND THE SURROUNDING AREA

CHARLESTON
East Bay B&B
301 East Bay Street
Charleston 29401
(843) 722-4186

King's B&B
198 King Street
Charleston 29401
(843) 723-7000

Rutledge Victorian Inn
114 Rutledge Avenue
Charleston 29401
(843) 722-7551

Sword Gate Inn
111 Tradd Stret
Charleston 29401
(843) 723-8518

Thomas Lamboll House
19 King Street
Charleston 29401
(843) 723-3212

Zero Water Street
31 East Battery Street
Charleston 29401
(843) 723-2841

PLACES TO EAT IN CHARLESTON AND THE SURROUNDING AREA

CHARLESTON
Bowen's Island
1870 Bowen's Island Road
Charleston 29412
(843) 795-2757

Jestine's Kitchen
251 Meeting Street
Charleston 29401

Robert's of Charleston
182 East Bay Street
Charleston 29401
(843) 577-7565

S.N.O.B.
192 East Bay Street
Charleston 29401
(843) 723-3424

Sharky's Pizza
306 King Street
Charleston 29401
(843) 722-7200

MOUNT PLEASANT
J. Bistro
819 Coleman Boulevard
Mount Pleasant 29464
(843) 971-1778

SULLIVAN'S ISLAND
Atlanticville Restaurant and Cafe
2063 Middle Street
Sullivan's Island 29482
(843) 883-9452

The Southern Corner

Barrier Islands

South of Charleston and all the way to Savannah, Georgia, 100 miles away, the land stays only a few feet above sea level and has a border of sandy barrier islands. Tall cypress trees rise above the live oaks and long-leaf pines, and the rivers feeding into the inlets and the ocean are a dark tea color, owing to the tannic acid from the cypress and swamp roots. In the narrow strip of lowland along the coast is the subtropical growth in which are found such plants as the large palmetto, several dwarf palmettos, yucca, and evergreen holly. The grasses along the coast are panicum, water millet, and sea oats, all of which are necessary to sustain the life of the rolling dunes protecting the shoreline from wind and tidal erosion. The people along Route 17, working small truck farms and commuting to Charleston and Hilton Head for work, have changed very little in the last hundred years.

As you travel on Route 17, especially on the long section south of Charleston, you'll be traveling through a part of the South that has withstood much of the tides of change. For a deeper insight and appreciation you might read *Praying for Sheetrock* by Melissa Fay Greens. In a wonderful storytelling style, she tells of the old road and captures much of the African-American culture marvelously.

Before you begin a tour of the Edisto Island area, which is this chapter's first destination, here's a little history. In 1666 Robert Sandford's British expedition dropped anchor at Edisto Island and spent a pleasant week with the Edistow Indians. They were helpful, cordial, and friendly, and the delighted Sandford went back to London and spread the news that this was the ideal place for a British colony. While he was gone, the Edistows had second thoughts. When the settlers returned, the Edistows told them they had changed their minds about tourists settling among them and that the natives up in Kiawah country a few miles north were

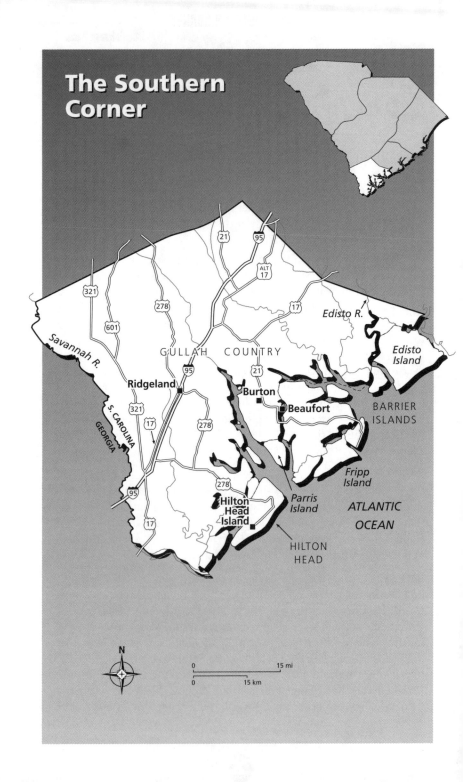

The Southern Corner

Savannah R.

S. CAROLINA

GEORGIA

GULLAH COUNTRY

Edisto R.

Edisto Island

BARRIER ISLANDS

Ridgeland

Burton

Beaufort

Fripp Island

ATLANTIC OCEAN

Parris Island

Hilton Head Island

HILTON HEAD

N

0   15 mi
0   15 km

Author's Favorite Places

Edisto Museum
(Edisto Island)

Bay Street Bookstore
(Beaufort)

Rhett House
(Beaufort)

Red Piano Too
(Route 21 at Frogmore)

Sheldon Church Ruins
(Route 21 near
Gardens Corner)

African Village
(Near Sheldon)

not only much friendlier but were actually looking for newcomers and would welcome them with open arms. The settlers got the message, weighed anchor, sailed back up the coast, and settled Charleston on the banks of the Ashley River.

In 1674 Edisto Island was purchased from the Indians by the Earl of Shaftsbury. Shortly after, Paul Grimball was granted 600 acres of land on the North Edisto River and built a plantation house. In 1686, Spanish marauders sacked the area and the plantation and destroyed the **Grimball Plantation.** Today, the remains of the foundation (made of tabby, which is a cement made of lime, sand or gravel, and crushed oyster shells) can still be seen near the river.

One hundred years before the British, the Spanish built a small mission here on the banks of St. Peire's Creek. Called "Oristo," a variant on the Indian word *Edistow,* the mission was operated by members of the Jesuit Order. Today, only a single place name, Spanish Mount Point, recalls that period more than 300 years ago.

Not far from the ruins of the Grimball Plantation at **Point of Pines** is an old graveyard of the early settlers. Unfortunately, the slate gravestones have worn smooth over the years and are barely legible, but if you look close you can see some of the dates are before 1700.

The Edisto Island Historic Preservation Society runs **The Edisto Museum** located at 2343 Highway 176, Edisto Island 29438. Each room is crowded with displays, books, old letters, and artifacts that trace the history of the island from the time of the Edistow Indians. One of the many attractions is an electronically controlled nature board on which you match animal prints to the animals. Kids love this; adults are baffled and generally give up fast. The museum is open only on Tuesday, Thursday, and Saturday from 1:00 to 4:00 P.M. Admission is $2.00 for adults; free for children ten and younger. Private tours can be arranged by calling the above numbers.

Across the driveway into the museum is a small pond where two resident alligators usually can be seen taking the morning sun. Note: Keep kids and small dogs away from them. A fact no one seems to believe is that alligators have remarkable speed for 20 to 30 yards and have been known to do terrible damage to dogs, deer, children, and slow-witted adults.

Alligator News

If the approximate distance from the eyes to the tip of the nose is 8 inches, that means the gator is 8 feet long. Ten inches means 10 feet, and so on. And one more tip: they actually love marshmallows. If you feel you have to feed them, do it from the bridges. And one last tip—DON'T.

Another hazard down here in the Low Country is snakes! Keep the children away from creek banks, drain ditches, heavy leaf-covered areas, and woods. South Carolina has the distinction of having the biggest variety of poisonous snakes in the country. As a matter of fact, Beaufort County, a few miles south of Edisto, is the place where most of the snakes used for extracting venom for snakebite serum are captured. They are also gathered for carnival shows as well as for a sprinkling of Pentecostal churches that still practice snake handling, or "snake chunking."

None of the snakes will attack unprovoked, but if you step on one or scare one, *that* is a different story. Some of the coral snakes are especially lethal. Beautiful and tiny with exquisite red and yellow bands, they look like toys, but as the locals say, "they can kill you quicker than a train." This is an exaggeration, but an untreated bite can be very dangerous. How do you tell a lethal coral snake from nonlethal? Simple rule:

YELLOW ON BLACK, FRIENDLY JACK.

BLACK ON YELLOW, WILL KILL A FELLOW.

Edisto, they say, is not so much a place as it is a time—and a time, preservationists add, that has resisted change. The old plantation money was made from indigo and sea-island cotton. Since enormous labor was needed for planting, tending, and harvesting these crops, the island became a major entry point for slaves from Africa and Barbados. The landowners sought out and secured the most educated slaves, and since many came from African aristocracy, race relations here were much different than they were in the rest of the state. Incidentally, the single-room-wide house construction in Charleston comes directly from Barbados.

One of the oldest stories here is of the very young white girl Hepzibah Jenkins, who was raised by local slaves when her mother died and her father was imprisoned in the Revolution. Later she married the island's largest landowner. Years passed, and in 1810 Hepzibah decided she wanted to build the plantation slaves a Baptist church. This inflamed her husband and the result was their separation. But Hepzibah was undaunted and started baking bread in a tabby oven (constructed of sea shells, lime, and sand) at what became the Hepzibah Jenkins Bakery. She financed and built the first church in America founded by a woman. The old bakery eventually disintegrated and became over-

Hurricane and Tornado Facts

A hurricane test: If you hold up a sheet of plywood to a window and turn it loose and it sticks, hammer it in and head for a shelter.

A test to see if you're in a hurricane: Check the rain—when it hits your window it will flow up and not down. This is hard to believe until you see it. But if you do see it, it's too late.

During a hurricane, most fish and all shrimp go crazy and swim in circles, even leap in the air. Some of the smart ones, however, swallow rocks and sink to the bottom.

Birds fly low to the ground. Some get caught in the eye and stay in it until the storm diminishes and thus wind up thousands of miles from home. Legend has it the snowy egret came from Africa in a hurricane eye.

Dogs howl and run around in tight little dog circles. Horses get nervous and stamp the ground. Cats ignore it.

If you're in a mobile home, get out in a hurry.

If you're on the road, and you shouldn't be, don't stay in the car. Find the nearest concrete culvert and crawl, climb, or claw your way under and stay there.

If the eye comes over, keep in mind that the worst part may very well be on its way. This is especially true if you are in the 12-to-3 quadrant of the hurricane. Keep in mind the hurricane is spinning counterclockwise. This means the wind behind it—say it's at 30 miles an hour—pushes it 30 miles faster in the 12-to-3 quadrant and slows it down 30 miles in the 6-to-9.

But don't take time to analyze this; get out of your car, stay out of mobile homes, and find that culvert.

The big killer in hurricanes down here is not the wind or the water but the locals who plug in home generators and forget to disconnect the outside line. What happens is someone will assume the line is dead and step on it or pick it up. Another killer, almost as lethal, is chain saws. If you use one make sure you don't under any conditions hold it above your head, and be absolutely certain your feet are planted firmly on something solid. You might also leave the beer in the car.

Tornadoes usually ride along on the edge of the hurricane and do tremendous damage. Since you won't be able to see them, there's no point in even watching for them. Just know they're out there and take every precaution.

For years churches were routinely destroyed during tornadoes, while the town saloons remained untouched. Finally a saloon keeper told a preacher to keep the church doors open the way he did. The preacher tried it and it worked. The word spread, and now churches and buildings of any kind leave their windows open when the storms threaten. So, wherever you're staying, crack your windows on each end when the storm warnings are announced.

Practical tip: Toss a few plastic gallon milk jugs (with tops) in your trunk. After a hurricane or a tornado they'll be worth their weight in gold for collecting and storing drinking water.

OFF THE BEATEN PATH

grown with vegetation, but the church, which is still called the Baptist Church, can be seen on the left side of Highway 174 as you enter Edisto. At the back of the church is the **grave of Hepzibah Jenkins,** and over it her children have erected a monument which reads:

> HER CHARACTER WAS SO STRONGLY CAST, AND HER IMPULSES WERE SO GENEROUS, THAT SHE WAS AN OBJECT OF INDIFFERENCE TO NO ONE. THE POOR AND THE AFFLICTED WERE SPECIAL OBJECTS OF HER CONSIDERATION. BY THEM HER LOSS IS TRULY FELT, AND BY US WHO KNEW HER BEST, SHE IS MOST LAMENTED.

Another incident that illustrates the tenacity and independence of the Edisto people occurred in 1861. It was then, when South Carolina was debating whether or not to sign the Ordinance of Secession, that the Edisto Island delegate jumped to his feet and declared that irrespective of what the State did, Edisto Island would secede from the Union all by itself.

In 1810 vacationers from Charleston and Columbia began coming to the Edisto beaches. That same year Edingsville Island was developed by one of the island's wealthy cotton planters, William Edings. By 1820 he had built sixty large summer cottages and a boardwalk; the resort was comparable to Atlantic City, New Jersey, or Newport, Rhode Island. Photographs of ladies with hoop skirts and parasols and men in skimmers can be seen in the Edisto Museum. Unfortunately, the hurricane of 1890

Travel Tips

T *here is something truly sad about sitting in an air-conditioned car, biting into what you think is an egg or chicken salad sandwich, and tasting the damage done by three to five hours on the road. Take my advice, you really don't have to live like that.*

One of my favorite sandwiches on the road is fresh egg or chicken salad with crisp bacon, lettuce, and mayonnaise on a heavy-duty whole-wheat bread. But, and it's a big but, after an hour or so inside a wrapper the bread picks up most of the moisture and breaks down. You might as well be eating tuna fish. I played golf in the Crosby Invitational last year and Yogi Berra, of all people, showed me how they handle egg salad up in a place called the Bronx. You take the top slice of bread off and stack the egg or chicken salad with about an inch of thick cut potato chips. Then you place the top slice back on, and after taking a firm grip on everything you're in business. Now you talk about winner! This is it! If you don't believe me, try it at home before you start traveling. You'll never eat another soggy sandwich.

32

destroyed everything standing, and the island returned to its formerly barren state as the barrier island it had been. It wasn't until 1994 that a new house was built here. The Atwood Agency on Highway 174 (call 843–863–2151) is currently handling the rental of that home.

Highway 174 dead-ends at Palmetto Drive. At the corner is *The Pavilion* restaurant, 102 Palmetto Boulevard, Edisto Island 29438, open for lunch and dinner six days a week, closed Tuesday. Good buys here are an all-you-can-eat shrimp dinner for $15.95. Beer and wine are served. Children are welcome and can be turned loose to walk along the beach. Call (843) 869–3061.

Dave Lybrand owns and helps operate the Edisto Sales and Rentals Realty at 1405 Palmetto Drive, Edisto Island 29438. Call (800) 868–5398 for reservations for beachfront houses and villas, and also creekside rentals. The variety of accommodations here is enormous. The Ocean Villa is rustic and right smack on the beach. The top floor has a huge porch overlooking the ocean where you can sunbathe, eat, drink, and be merry as you watch the long strings of pelicans gliding down the beach. I stayed here last year and counted eighty-six brown pelicans in one group. They often number over a hundred. Private homes also are available for weekly rental. A beachfront house that sleeps eight averages $1,800 per week; houses off the beach range from about $600 to $1,200.

Coming into Edisto is the *Old Post Office,* 1442 Highway 174, Edisto Island 29438, the premier restaurant on the island. The menu includes shrimp broiled with a mousseline sauce on whole-grained grits at $17 and a pecan-coated quail for the same price. A three-course dinner for two with wine should run you around $90. The coproprietor and chef, Philip Bardin, is a native here and can whip up the best southern fare in the Low Country. The Old Post Office serves dinner only; reservations are required. Dress is casual. Closed Sunday. Open Monday–Saturday, from May 1 through September and Tuesday–Saturday, October through April. Call (843) 869–2339.

Edisto Island, with more than 7 miles of uninterrupted beach, has managed to keep its landscape, skyline, and ecology about the way they were twenty or thirty years ago. It's still one of the real jewels on the South Carolina coastline. It's also one of the best areas in the entire country for collecting fossils. This is because this coastline was once a lengthy primordial bog, and today the tides and currents keep stirring it up. Shark's teeth are easy to find, but they are nothing when compared to the fossils of some of the creatures that inhabited the area millions of years ago. Along these shores have been found the remains of elephants with tusks turned backwards, crocodiles 30 feet long, a 200-pound capybara (the biggest rodent in the world), birds with teeth and 19-foot wingspans, a ground sloth as big as a Volkswagen, horses with three toes, camels, tapirs, and saber-toothed tigers. Many invertebrate paleontologists still refer to the 1857 *Pliocene Fossils of South Carolina,* by Francis Holmes and Michael Tuomey, as the classic book about this science in the state.

"Anything new I acquire I keep close for a few days," says Don Marvin, a retired architect and vocational fossil hunter here on the island. "It's like having a brand-new toy." Marvin and his wife, Gracie, became fossil hunters after years of collecting shark's teeth. Today their collection is so vast they have created a museum on the bottom floor of their home on Jungle Road. It is probably one of the largest private collections on the East Coast. If nothing else, it proves that Edisto Beach was home to the stout-legged llama and the beautiful armadillo. Don and Gracie's **Fossil Hunter's Museum** at 606 Jungle Shore Drive, Edisto Island 29438, is open to visitors by appointment only, no charge. Call (843) 869–3435.

South Carolina's mountains-to-the-sea terrain is the geological feature that has made fossil hunting so good down here. As the Appalachian Mountains eroded, sediments washed downhill. Water from the ocean, which at one time came all the way up to Columbia, carried minerals that fossilized plants and animals. The result has been an incredible resource for the paleontologists of today. Al Sanders, the curator of natural sciences at The Charleston Museum, says, "When you can see and hold and touch something tangible from something as bizarre in the human experience as dinosaurs, then I think you're a little broader person for it."

He recalls seeing the fossils of a bird found near the Charleston air base in 1984. It was the world's second-largest known flying bird, with a wingspan of 19 feet. "If you can't get excited about that, there's something wrong with you," Al says.

Fairfield Ocean Ridge is a 350-acre resort with one-, two-, and three-bedroom villas for rent by the night or the week. Call (843) 869–2561. Golf packages can be arranged for playing the **Edisto Beach Country Club** (call 843–869–1111). The course is right on the property; many of the villas overlook the fairways. As a matter of fact, you can step out on the fairway with a nine iron and a bag of balls and get in all the practice you need. The green fees and cart rentals are the lowest in the entire area, which is a notable fact since this is a 6,300-yard absolutely first-class course with wonderful greens and enough tight fairways to give any golfer all the challenge he or she needs. As a matter of cold fact, water comes into play on fourteen holes, and I'd suggest a long iron, rather than a wood, from many of the tees. The Tom Jackson–designed course is owned and operated by Jim and Patti Herrin, both golf enthusiasts, and they are doing a remarkable job keeping it in shape year-round.

Unlike most country clubs, where you have to know someone before you are allowed to pay—usually more than $100—to play, tee times here are unbelievably easy to arrange. All you have to do is show up at the pro shop with plenty of balls. For the golfer whose spouse doesn't play, this is probably the best course in the state where you can take him/her out for a lesson and have a great time doing it. Between the greens and tees are some wonderful walks through the live oaks, palmettos, and magnolia trees. *Caution:* When you walk near the lakes and creeks, keep your eyes peeled for the local alligators and an occasional snake. Armadillos, who have been spotted here recently, are harmless. This is also a wonderful spot for bird-watching; you're sure to see three or four great blue herons and all the brown pelicans you can count. If your spouse doesn't play, take him/her with you anyway for the cart ride through this really wonderful and unique area. The country club has an excellent restaurant between the ninth green and the tenth tee. One final suggestion: If you're planning on playing here, use the driving range at the other end of the island to warm up.

At the north end of the beach is **Edisto Beach State Park.** Though small, the campground is one of the prettiest in the state. Many of the sites are set on small hills under live oaks and look out on the ocean only a few yards away. The campground is equipped with electrical and water hookups, barbecue pits, and a place to shower. A grocery store is only a block away. For those who love to camp or for folks on a budget that won't allow resort rates, this is the ideal place to stay. While here you can explore the nature trails or go fishing, crabbing, or sailing. It is also an excellent place for bird-watching. For further information write Edisto Beach State Park, Highway 174, Edisto Island 29438 or call (843) 869–2156.

For an elaborate rental house that is truly off the beaten path, call the Prudential Kapp/Lyons Agency at (843) 869–2516 or (800) 945–9667 and ask for information on Bucky Battle's house, **Whitmarsh,** at the end of Botany Road. The road is canopied by a beautiful tunnel of live oaks shrouded with Spanish moss; it was used in the movie *Ace Ventura Pet Detective Part Two.* So, if you like, you can check out the movie and see where the Battle house is located.

The house has six bedrooms and three and a half baths; it can sleep as many as fourteen. The price is $1,695 per week in season, $1,295 off-season. The house, completely secluded and overlooking Frampton Inlet and the ocean, stands more than 40 feet high and, with its 180-degree view, has probably the best vista on the island. You can sit in the cocktail area at the top of the house and watch the leaping porpoises as they follow the shrimp boats into port in the afternoons. You will also see pelicans, egrets, heron, ospreys, ducks, geese, and even eagles. In the pastures off Botany Road you can see egrets doing something rather strange. One egret will ride on a cow's back and pick off fleas while two others high-step along in the grass eating the crickets and grasshoppers the cow flushes up. A little more bird lore here: When you visit the Lyons Agency, look out the side window at the birdfeeder, where a pair of Low Country Painted Buntings are trying to build a nest. This is a very rarely-sighted bird. With its blues, yellows, reds, and greens, it looks a great deal like a parrot straight out of the Amazons, only smaller.

You should also know that Edisto is a fishing paradise. You can fish here on the beach, from the creek banks, or from a john boat. John boats and surfing equipment can be rented for a nominal charge at **The Marina,** and you can fish almost anywhere you choose. Many local residents simply cast their lines from the bridges into the creeks or the inlets. Fishing here, you'll meet some of the resident characters of the island, and you'll get enough fishing advice to last a lifetime. One line you might hear from someone speaking Gullah is, "Most hook fish don' hep dry hominy," which means "The fish you almost caught doesn't do much for a plate of grits."

As you fish and watch the colors changing on the marsh grass and a long string of pelicans heading home right above you, you might consider what I. Jenkins Mikell, a plantation owner down here, once said. "Life here is one long dream. Here the art of being busy and doing nothing was brought to a fine point."

Leave Edisto on Highway 174, go to Route 17, and turn left to Gardens Corner, roughly 15 miles away back on the mainland. The land here remains about the same—low and sandy with pine trees, magnolia, and a dozen varieties of oak. Turn left on Route 21. Only 5 miles down the road is **Beaufort,** the second oldest town in the state, settled in 1711. During the Civil War the town was occupied by the Union forces, which saved it from being burned. Today the big homes looking out over the inlet and the ocean are almost exactly as they were in 1860. You can get a very good idea of the look of the old town and its surroundings from any one of the following movies filmed here: *Glory, The Big Chill, The Great Santini, Forrest Gump, Conrack,* and *Prince of Tides.* As a matter of fact, Pat Conroy (author of *Prince of Tides)* spent his childhood here and later taught school down the coast out on Daufuskie Island. And as another matter of fact, the cast of *Prince of Tides*—Barbra Streisand, Nick Nolte, and Jeroen Krabbé—all stayed downtown at Rhett House, one of the old mansions that have been converted to a bed-and-breakfast inn. More on that later.

Your first stop should be the ***Visitor Information Center*** at 1006 Bay Street, Beaufort 29902; the phone number is (843) 524–3163. Here you can pick up a walking-tour map with points of particular interest marked out. They will also help you with suggestions for restaurants and places to stay if you are spending the night, which you should do. Mornings here on Bay Street, with its very large and very beautifully landscaped park that runs along the waterfront, are wonderful. The park backs up to restaurants, coffee shops, and the very well-run ***Bay Street Bookstore,*** which not only sells current books and best-sellers but also local books, local recipes, and the famous ghost books for which the area is known.

If you feel like walking a few miles, pick up a tour map and just follow the dotted lines. The map shows twenty-six historical sites, including ***St. Helena's Episcopal Church,*** built in 1724, and the 1840 ***George Elliott Museum,*** which was a Federal hospital during the Civil War. If you're not too keen on walking, a much easier way of seeing the old town is from the seat of one of the very comfortable horse-drawn carriages that are parked at the curb and available at almost any hour. Prices run around $15 per half hour. If you are so inclined, take the ride right around sundown with an iced bottle of white wine.

At 1009 Craven Street, Beaufort 29902, is the aforementioned and internationally famous ***Rhett House.*** This is the ideal place to stay in Beaufort, but you must make your reservations early. Actors, directors, and writers have been headquartering at this centerpiece long before *The Big Chill* was filmed in this area. The inn's hosts, Steve and Marianne Harrison, originally from New York, have a marvelous collection of candid photographs of Streisand, Nick Nolte, and Jeroen Krabbé all looking delighted with their accommodations and everything around them. Check the kitchen and ask the cook to show you the fascinating print that Jeroen Krabbé gave the Harrisons.

This old mansion, which is as ornamental as a wedding cake, has wraparound verandas, classic columns and porticos, and beautifully

Rhett House, Beaufort

carved and finished entries and staircases. Fresh flowers are everywhere, and each and every appointment is in excellent taste. Every room has a small library; the main library has everything from Nabokov to Stephen King to Jackie Collins. All guest rooms have televisions, telephones, and private baths; two have fireplaces. You can even sleep in the same bed that Barbra Streisand slept in. The management will be glad to arrange golf, tennis, swimming, and massages. Carriage tours, sunset cruises, and historic walks are also available. Rates are $125 to $225. Call (843) 524–9030.

Steve and Marianne are delightful and knowledgeable company and love to talk far into the night on books, the theater, and the movies. The excellent gourmet dinners here feature regional favorites such as crab cakes, fresh fish, roast lamb, and vegetables with herbs from the Rhett House gardens. You can even dine on the porch under the limbs of the great live oak in the front yard. On Sunday evenings the Harrisons offer elegant supper baskets as a dinner alternative. Room rates include not only wonderful accommodations but afternoon teas, bicycles, and a full breakfast. Smoking is limited to the porches, verandas, and garden.

Two blocks from Rhett House at 906 Port Republic Street, Beaufort 29902, is a little gem of a restaurant called *Emily's.* Featuring a unique menu that includes twenty-nine different dishes called tapas, this is a spot that should not be overlooked. Just a few of the exotic dishes that represent the international flavor of the place are escargot Bourguignon, wild boar sausage, crabmeat Rangoon, and tempura shrimp. Emily's also has an excellent wine list. The bar at the end of the room is perfect for meeting a few of the more interesting local residents. Dress is casual. Open from 4:30 to 11:00 P.M. Monday through Saturday. Call (843) 522–1866 for reservations.

The *Two-Suns Inn* at 1705 Bay Street, Beaufort 29902, is a restored neoclassical Revival-style home that once served as a home for female teachers living and working here in Beaufort. Today it is a bed-and-breakfast and houses the weaving studio of innkeeper Carol Kay. Rates here are $105 and up. Call (843) 522–1122.

Four or five blocks away at 910 Bay Street, Beaufort 29902, is **Banana's,** which is about what it sounds like. The staff here call the place "the fun spot on the waterfront" and recommend you show up in shorts or jeans. Banana's serves hot dogs, homemade potato chips, eight different kinds of sandwiches, and nine kinds of half-pound burgers. If you're in the mood, you can order steak, ribs, or fresh shrimp. All meals are served with homemade bread. Prices range from $10 to $25. It's a great place to eat and linger and watch the locals watching the tourists and the tourists watching the locals. Open 11:00 A.M. to 10:00 P.M., seven days a week. The restaurant features live entertainment Thursday to Sunday. Call (843) 522–0910.

If you drive a few miles down Bay Street you'll see the signs to **Parris Island;** follow them. Unlike most military bases, which discourage visitors, this active Marine Corps base welcomes them. Visitors may take a driving tour of the island; the tour leads through the old Navy yard and to the site of the Spanish forts that were here in the seventeenth century. You can also visit the War Memorial Building on the base. Here you can see exhibits on the history and development of Parris Island and the history of the Marine Corps. The island is open year-round, Monday through Friday from 7:00 A.M. to 4:30 P.M. and on Saturday, Sunday, and holidays from 9:00 A.M. to 4:30 P.M. Call (843) 525–2951.

Leave Beaufort and head out over the Lady's Island Bridge for **Fripp Island,** about 25 miles away. The islands get confusing here—Lady's, Pritchards, Hunting, and then Fripp all stem off Route 21. Just follow the signs and you can't go wrong.

A half-mile from Beaufort, turn right at Whitehall Drive to the **Whitehall Plantation.** This is a superb lunch and dinner spot in the middle of a beautiful garden of cassina hedges, camellias, live oaks, cedars, and a natural bamboo forest. With the help of folks with a fine appreciation of history and beauty, this waterfront piece of land has been preserved and improved over the years and now houses one of the finest restaurants in the area. I had a great meal here of crab cakes and fried shrimp with an excellent salad. Best of all was a thick slice of Southern Chocolate Cake with a cocoa pecan frosting. Prices range from $18 to $27 for dinner. Special menu for kids under twelve. Lunch is served from 11:30 A.M. to 2:30 P.M., dinner from 5:30 to 9:00 P.M. Closed Sunday and Monday. Call (843) 521–1700.

Gullah Country

Heading for the end of Fripp Island on Route 21, you'll pass through the tiny village of **St. Helena Island,** which is probably the center of the Gullah culture and language. These inhabitants of the South Carolina coast are the only group of African-Americans who have been able to trace their roots to the villages of the Sierra Leone territory in West Africa. This heritage is evidenced most dramatically in the rice agriculture, cast-net fishing, and arts and crafts such as coiled basketry of these lowlands, as well as the language and the music.

A half-mile from the center of St. Helena Island is the **Penn Center Historic District.** This was the first school established in the South to educate the freed slaves. The center has sixteen buildings, including cottages for groups of up to 100 and a small museum dedicated to the language and culture of the blacks who were native to this region. Penn Center was designated a National Historic Landmark in 1974. For additional information on the events that take place here, write to Penn Center Historic District, P.O. Box 126, St. Helena Island 29920, or call (843) 838–2432. The museum is open Monday–Saturday from 11:00 A.M. until 4:00 P.M. Admission is $2 for children.

On Route 21 in the middle of St. Helena Island you'll find the **Red Piano Too,** Highway 21E, St. Helena Island 29920. It's impossible to miss and is certainly the most interesting art gallery in the entire Southeast. The building, for years a big grocery store, is a high-ceilinged wooden structure that has been on the National Register for some years now and is a one-of-a-kind masterpiece. Red Piano Too exhibits and sells African-American artwork that ranges in price from $5.00 to $1,500. Much of the work is done locally, and the imagination and craftsmanship are truly remarkable.

One of the artists to keep an eye on is Everett Mayo, a former heavyweight boxing champion from Virginia. He was headed for a promising career when a construction accident left him legally blind in one eye. Everett then allowed his longtime love for art to emerge, and he began channeling his creative energies toward painted sculpture. Each piece of his work is done on driftwood found on the local riverbanks, and on this he paints his string of unforgettable animals, from wolves to tigers to a 6-foot-high giraffe and a 7-foot-long shark.

Red Piano Too also sells postcards, prints, Bibles written in Gullah, and small hand-painted memorabilia. The gallery even has a Pat Conroy

Room where all of his books (autographed) are sold. If you are in Beaufort, or near Beaufort, or anywhere in South Carolina, this is a place you have to see. Call (843) 838–2241.

Continuing on toward Fripp Island on Route 21, try **The Shrimp Shack,** which features casual family dining on an outside porch. Prices here are in anybody's ballpark. For $8.50 you get a fried or boiled shrimp dinner with sides of red rice and coleslaw along with a Low Country "hush puppy," which is a deep-fried corn stick shaped like a torpedo. The name goes back to the time when the kitchens to the plantations were in the backyards, and the cooks would toss corn bread to the yapping dogs and say "hush now, puppy." No reservations are necessary, but if you want to call ahead for a take-out order call (843) 838–2962.

Gullah-n-Geechie Mahn Tours offers packages for bus tours as well as private van tours of the islands, where the Gullah culture is most apparent. You may choose tours that concentrate on such areas of interest as Gullah/Low Country cuisine (Low Country boil or oyster roast); cultural performances featuring storytelling unique to the Gullah culture, dance performances, plantation melodies, blues, and jazz; and crafts and demonstrations that include sweet grass basket weaving, crabbing, shrimping, and net making. They will also make arrangements for your overnight accommodations, fishing, boat rides, and beach and shopping excursions, as well as golf and tennis games. Tour hours are Monday–Friday 9:45 A.M. to 11:45 A.M., 1:45 to 3:45 P.M., and 4:30 to 6:30 P.M. Call (843) 838–7516 or (843) 838–6312, or write to P.O. Box 1248, St. Helena Island 29920.

Still on Route 21 heading for Fripp Island, stop at the **Gay Fish Incorporated,** 1948 Sea Island Parkway, St. Helena Island 29920, for fresh shrimp and fish by the pound or the hundredweight. Charlie Gay also sells spices for cooking shrimp, cookbooks, and marine supplies. Eighteen boats dock at the pier here, and Charlie Gay says if you talk to one of the eighteen captains you will be able to make arrangements to go out on a shrimp run. Call (843) 838–2763. If you want to go, set the alarm clock. The boats leave at 4:00 A.M.

Continue on Route 21 toward Fripp Island. This will take you to **Hunting Island State Park,** one of South Carolina's most spectacular parks. Located at one end of the park is the Hunting Island Lighthouse, the only one of the seven South Carolina lighthouses open to the public. The beach here is ideal for shelling. For an extraordinary view of the entire area you can take a deep breath and climb the 181 steps to the top of the lighthouse.

Reservations can be made for rental cabins in the park. Write Hunting

Island State Park, 1775 Sea Island Parkway, St. Helena Island 29920, or call (843) 838–2011.

While parts of this extraordinary, smooth beach are reserved for swimming and surfing, other areas are used by surf fishermen. Comfort stations complete with showers are placed in several locations along the beach. The park also provides biking and nature trails. Open year-round from daybreak to dark.

As far as a lot of us down here in the Carolinas are concerned, the best and most accessible resort on the coast is *Fripp Island Resort.* Not only is it remote enough to qualify as "Off the Beaten Path," it has the perfect geography: a pristine beach on one side and a great sweep of tidal marshland on the other. Since tidal marshland cannot be developed, the resort will never get too big or too commercial or too anything. It's the perfect size. For an affordable resort Fripp has every amenity the larger resorts have but without the spread and the density and the impersonality that often comes with it.

For an idea of what the beach and the live oak and Spanish Moss landscape looks like, pick up videos of two recent movies that were shot here: *Forrest Gump* and Disney's *The Jungle Book.*

When you rent a one-, two-, or three-bedroom condo or a beachfront house here, you automatically become a guest member of the Fripp Island Club and have full access to all of the resort facilities. Included in these are three top-notch golf courses. The latest, at Ocean Creek, was designed by Davis Love III and has been named one of the best new courses in the country by *Golf* magazine.

In addition to the three courses, the resort provides a "Wee Links" setup on each course. This consists of tee placements for kids where they can play from shorter yardages and still be on a championship course.

Travel Tips

*H*ere's a way to save money! Stop at the first rest stop in South Carolina and pick up a copy of the book of motel discount coupons. It's free. The lists are complete and come with detailed maps. In the current book some of the participating motels include Comfort Inn, Holiday Inn, Travelodge, Best Western, and so on. The motels and the rates may change from month to month but the coupon book will spell this out for you as well as give you a good idea of exactly where to find the bargains. In the current book eighty-five motels are listed, along with their rates and general information. Don't forget this.

THE SOUTHERN CORNER

The advantage here is that your child can play along with you.

Fripp Island Resort, keeping the family in mind, has also provided a children's play pool with an alligator slide and giant frog and a lagoon-style pool with caves and waterfalls. other facilities include croquet courts, a playground with a pirate ship, a basketball court, tennis facilities, and bike rentals. The tennis facilities are excellent, with eight soft courts and two hard courts. You can also rent skiffs, kayaks, or pontoon boats and take a trip on one of the beautiful creeks and waterways to watch for herons, ospreys, pelicans, and dolphins and explore the marshlands. Fishing tackle and crab and shrimp nets can be rented. Guided wildlife excursions are available for six passengers or less.

The food here at Fripp Island Resort ranges from excellent Low Country seafood and sizzling steaks served at the Ocean Grill Restaurant overlooking the ocean to hot dogs and ice cream at the sides of the three Olympic-size pools. Hugo's Cafe and Deli is famous for its pizza.

For the family that wants to live on or near the beach and wants to play golf or tennis, fish, crab, swim, and investigate the wildlife in a truly spectacular setting, Fripp Island resort is where you should be.

Since the rates vary with the season and what kind of rental you are looking for, you should contact the resort for current rates. Write Fripp Island Resort, One Tarpon Boulevard, Fripp Island, SC 29920 or call (800) 845–4100.

Fripp Island Marina is located out on the end of Route 21 on Fripp Island at 28 Salt Wind Drive, St. Helena Island 29920. Here you can fish from the 25-foot *Glory Halleluyah,* which can accommodate up to four guests. Captain Eddie supplies bait, tackle, ice, and all the instructions you need to make your trip first class. His "Grady White" type boat is fully equipped with the latest electronics, head, icebox, stereo, and full cabin. He specializes in trolling for mackerel, kingfish, amberjack, bonito, barracuda, cobia, dolphin, wahoo, and sailfish. A full day is priced at $500, a three-quarter day is $400, and half a day is $300. If you haven't tried this, it's a real thrill. Just bring sunblock and wear soft-soled shoes. Call (843) 838–3782.

From Fripp Island Marina go back through Beaufort on Route 21. As you leave Beaufort the kids will enjoy stopping to climb upon and take pictures of the three jet fighters poised for flight at the gates of the Marine Corps Air Station.

Sheldon Church Ruins, on Route 21 near Gardens Corner, is something truly off the beaten path. It's a beautiful old brick Episcopal church set in the middle of three or four huge live oaks with a cemetery at the side and in the back with tombstones dating back before 1700. The old church has been burned three times and during the last 300 years has probably never had a roof. But the simple brick columns still reach up and up into the Spanish moss, and the altar and front facade, highlighted with the sun streaming through the leaves, give it a grace and dignity that require nothing else. Sunrise services are held here every Easter morning; if you're within 100 miles, drive over—it will be an experience you will never forget.

Farther out Route 21, just before you hit I–95, are two spots the kids will like. The first is **Pocataligo,** which is the smallest town in the state. As reported earlier, the name is a short version of "poke a turtle's tail and he will go." The town is so small it has only one sign and the last population count was fewer than twelve. Natives joke that it's more of a place than a town. Tourists coming through often stop and back up and take a photograph of the sign.

Roadside Religion

A sign near Sheldon painted on a 4' x 8' piece of plywood beckons visitors to venture down "Safari Road" and visit the African Village founded in 1970 by King Oba Ofuntola Adelabu Adefunmi. The King, who has been on Oprah defending his right to practice polygamy, is a former used car dealer who was smart enough to see the tax benefits of starting not only his own religion ("New World Yoruba") but also his own country. Oyotunji is not part of the United States.

I have been here three times now, and each time I get a different version of what the King and his followers are doing. At one time they were living exclusively off the land in preparation to returning to Yoruba, their ancestral home. Recently they have been trying to attract the tourist trade, and today they offer guided tours of their village and their way of life. The last time I was here my guide was wearing a colorful dashiki and proudly showed me his decorative facial scars. He spoke in a rapid-fire singsong with many Yoruba words and glottal clicks thrown in and was worth the modest admission. Unfortunately, the "Royal Palace" where the King and his many wives reside looks as if it has seen better days. But if you're within 50 miles you should go here and listen to the drums and hear the pronouncements. It's harmless and safe and a place you'll never forget. You can also buy curious handmade mantelpiece items at rock-bottom prices. No phone. No pool. No pets.

Nearby is **Hobo Joe's,** which is next door to **Sad Sam's,** which is across the road from **Jolly Joe's.** Together, all three of these places look like a series of sideshows at a carnival. But they're not. This is the way we merchandise fireworks down here in the "hard lard belt." At any one of these places you can buy anything from penny firecrackers to bottle rockets to $50 ten-stage Roman candles that go as high as 500 feet. You can even buy $100 extravaganzas that fire one-hundred salvos and end with a Fourth of July celebration that looks not unlike the New York fireworks on the East River. This will be a great treat for the kids because South Carolina law not only allows you to buy these items over the counter but also allows you to take them out in any uninhabited field and fire away. Everybody does it. So get plenty of punk for lighting your explosives and have fun. Caution: Be sure to use long sticks of punk to light fireworks and make sure the fuse is sticking straight out. And don't hold exploding Roman candles.

Celebrity News
Watch for sign near Bluffton: WELCOME TO BLUFFTON, S.C. HOME OF JOE FRAZIER.

Hilton Head

The resident Indians here on Hilton Head fought off the settlements of the Spanish, the French, and the British until the middle of the 1700s, when they finally were overwhelmed by the British, who took over the area, introduced indigo, cotton, and rice, and started what was to become a boom economy that lasted until after the Civil War. Much hand labor was used to turn the leaves of the indigo plant into the cakes of blue dye that were in great demand at this time all around the world. Part of that labor involved stirring the steaming vats of foul-smelling indigo with long paddles. Slaves were imported from Barbados and later from Africa to accomplish this task and many others. When the slaves were freed after the Civil War, the planters left the island to them and went back to Charleston and inland to the Upcountry of South Carolina. The freed slaves now owned and worked the land and developed the Gullah culture with its own language, which is a mix of English, African dialects, and calypso-sounding French. It is wonderful to listen to once you get the hang and rhythm of it.

In the twentieth century the island's climate and beautiful beaches began attracting developers who began buying land on the island. Slowly but inexorably, the blacks, with their rich Gullah tradition, were forced to leave the land. Many of them work today in service jobs on Hilton Head Island, and a few own small businesses there, but many have moved to the mainland around Bluffton. Luckily much of the Gullah tradition is still present here and can be seen in the Low Country cuisine, arts, music, and language.

Today Hilton Head has much to offer the tourist. The main attractions are the greatest concentration of outstanding golf courses, tennis facilities, fishing marinas, and accommodations in the country. All twenty-five golf courses are on the big island and neighboring Daufuskie Island. A few courses are private and thus for members only, but most are available for guests of the hotels and villas.

The winters are very mild here, but the ocean water is still very cold. You can't go swimming in the ocean, unless you do it for a very few seconds, but you can play golf and tennis, ride bikes, go for nature walks, and go deep-sea fishing and sailing almost every day of the year.

The MCI Heritage Golf Tournament in mid-April is internationally famous and is played on the weekend after the Masters Tournament in Augusta, Georgia, right across the South Carolina border. Tickets for the Heritage are usually available, and it is one of those rare tournaments where you can actually walk right along the course with your favorite professional.

Palmetto Dunes is perhaps the ideal spot on Hilton Head to bring a sports-minded family. This 2,000-acre resort has three championship golf courses, the nationally acclaimed Rod Laver Tennis Center, a deep-water marina, and more than 3 miles of uninterrupted beach. Uninterrupted here means that sometimes you won't see a single soul for a mile. For reservations and information write P.O. Box 5606, Highway 278, Hilton Head 29928, or call (843) 785–1138.

Backroads You Don't Want to Be Out on Too Late at Night

*R*oute 275 out of Harleyville is a two-lane blacktop winding through a part of the old Palmetto State that may never change. IMPEACH EARL WARREN has faded badly on the smooth rocks and run-off culverts but GET US OUT OF THE U.N. is still with us in fresh spray paint, along with directions for where to buy night crawlers, crickets, and she-crab soup, and where you can get a good head, palm, or root reading. One sign in tortured hand lettering outside Bluffton—the area that gave the world Father Devine, Reverend Ike, Joe Frazier and recently Del Webb—looks as if it has been lifted from The Guinness Book of World Records: "Man has gotten away with more sin and unrighteousness during the past twenty years than during any period since God drove Adam and Eve from the Garden of Eden."

While there is a Palmetto Dunes Club private membership, and the feeling is definitely of a private club, all three courses here and the tennis courts are open year-round to the public. Guests at the Hyatt Hotel and the Mariner's Inn here at Palmetto Dunes are given preferential tee times and reduced rates. Incidentally, these are the golf courses President Clinton plays every spring when he comes to the island for the Renaissance Convention.

While the Hyatt and the Mariner's Inn are stunning places to stay, many prefer the more informal villas, which are ideal for families. The villas as a group are like a giant two-story hotel spread around twenty-five pools; the result is that every three or four villas have semi-private swimming.

You can rent a two- or three-bedroom villa facing the tennis courts, one of the golf courses, or the ocean. You can even rent one on a stream with a free canoe tossed in. If you have enough Scout merit badges, you can pack your golf clubs or tennis racket carefully in the middle of the canoe and paddle to the course or the court. The villas come equipped with wonderful kitchens; supermarket shopping is less than a mile away. If you're traveling with children you can use the babysitting and day-care facilities here, and if the kids are turned loose on the ocean or at one of the pools, there are plenty of well-trained lifeguards. The villas offer a unique combination of privacy and convenience to the golf courses, tennis courts, supermarkets, and a mall of outlet stores.

While Hilton Head may appear to be crowded in the high season—spring and fall—Palmetto Dunes is set way back from the main road and the traffic is completely off the beaten path. As a result, the resort offers as much isolation as you want.

Alligators up to 14 feet long thrive among the creeks and lakes here at Palmetto Dunes, as do raccoons, deer, and an occasional red fox. In the evening, possums pad from one house to the next looking for handouts. If you stand still long enough at night, there's a good chance of seeing one of the four or five native owls. Bird-watching here is like no place in the country. Audubon Society members, who come here often, have recorded more than 120 species in the immediate area. Watch for the painted bunting, the indigo bunting, the osprey, and the skimmer bird who glides along flashing its red head to attract the fish, then makes a 180-degree turn and comes back and scoops them up with the lower part of its bill. The bird only operates when the water is calm. But watch for them, they're out there.

Harbour Town, located around the rim of Calibogue Sound, is domi-nated by the candy-striped *Hilton Head Lighthouse.* The cove, with its ninety-odd-slip yacht basin, is home for the serious boaters who travel the Intracoastal Waterway. A pleasant pastime here is to sit on one of the many rocking chairs with a drink or an ice cream cone or nothing and watch the boats coming in as the sun sets. If you've watched the Heritage Classic Golf Tournament on television, this area will look familiar. Surrounding the cove is a series of upscale shops, restaurants, and condominiums.

Directly across from the cove is the *Heritage Grill,* located in the club-house of the Harbour Town Golf Links. This small grill looks out over the ninth hole of the course and the putting green. The grill is open daily for breakfast and lunch. Dinner is offered Wednesday through Sunday. Call (843) 671–3119 for reservations.

Also near the lighthouse in Harbour Town is the fashionable *Cafe Europa,* at 160 Lighthouse Road, Hilton Head, 29928, which is open for breakfast from 9:00 to 11:00 A.M. Monday through Friday, 9:00 A.M. to noon on weekends, for lunch from 11:00 A.M. to 2:30 P.M. daily, and for dinner from 5:30 to 10:00 P.M. daily. Call (843) 671–3399.

Ron Cerudo and Doug Weaver, two of the best pros that ever played on the PGA Tour, are now in residence at *Shipyard Plantation* (telephone 843–290–6726) where they give group instructions. Both Ron and Doug have won some of the biggest tournaments in the country. Today they are rated with the best of the best as instructors of the game. Both feel that amateurs' main problems stem from their setup, grip, and stance, and they believe every lesson should begin by working on these basics.

They are both excellent in short-game management and believe the basic chip and run should be a great deal like the putting stroke. They also believe in changing amateurs' basic swing as little as possible and trying to get them to believe in tempo and balance.

Rates are $80 for 45 minutes; kids twelve and under, $50.

Back on U.S. 278 at the Gateway to Hilton Head is the *Low Country Factory Outlet Village,* 1414 Fording, Bluffton 29910. This mall, with more than forty name-brand merchants, is the area's largest outlet shopping center. Some of the brands are Eddie Bauer, J. Crew, and Polo. Call (843) 837–4339.

When you tire of golf and shopping, head for *Reilly's Grill and Bar,* 7D

Greenwood Drive, Hilton Head Plaza, Hilton Head 29928. Call (843) 842–4414. Very popular for lunch and dinner, it's a combination grill, bar, sports bar, and hangout. Several televisions are always honed in on whatever sports event is in the air. Hamburgers and fries are especially good here, as are the coffee and desserts. The average lunch will cost you about $8.00; you can spend more for dinner, but try the burger first. The waitresses are friendly and funny. This is a great place to have a beer and watch the local action. There's a very good chance you'll come back. Open seven days a week from 11:00 A.M. to 11:30 P.M.

A few words about alligators on Hilton Head and all over the Low Country. I played golf here with a comic named Kenny Davis who had never been north of Tahoe or east of Vegas. He had never been to a zoo, and the only alligators he had ever seen were in the movies. I told him I could guarantee that he would see at least a dozen when we played golf on Hilton Head.

Well, we teed off, and perhaps the cloud cover was too thick or too thin or the pollen count was wrong, but for some reason we didn't see a single gator—only egrets, pelicans, doves, and an occasional pileated woodpecker. Finally, on the seventeenth hole, long after Kenny had decided that there was no such thing as an alligator, there beside a lagoon lay a monster that looked longer than my Ford.

Kenny looked at it and began laughing. It was so big and looked so ridiculous and was so asleep, he thought it was something plastic up from Disney World that I'd had some redneck buddy blow up for his benefit. Before I could stop him he was prodding the beast with his putter. And then two strange events happened simultaneously. The alligator's mouth opened, and the monster rose up in a hissing, rushing lunge. Kenny did a quickstep and levitated 2 or 3 feet, straight up. He did some aerial acrobatics, hit the ground running, and didn't turn around until he was 100 yards down the fairway. He was no longer laughing. Yes, Virginia, there are alligators down here.

If you're this far south, you might as well take another half hour and go on down Route 17 to Savannah, Georgia. Next to Charleston, at least for me, this is the most beautiful city in the country. Right in the center of the old town on the corner of Jones and Jefferson, and looking like a warehouse, is Johnny Mercer's old hangout *The Crystal Beer Parlor.* Photos of Mercer, who wrote "Georgia," "Moon River," "Skylark," "Tangerine," "Laura," and about 100 other songs, are all over the place. The big, red leather booths are wonderful to sit in, the waiters are great, and the food is superb. Try the cheeseburger or the shrimp salad. Best of all, for something truly unforgettable, try the fried oyster sandwich. Prices range from $7.00 to $14.00. The Crystal is open Monday through Saturday from 11:00 A.M. to 8:30 P.M. and 11:00 A.M. to 9:00 P.M. Friday and Saturday. Closed Sundays. Call (912) 232–1153. While you are here, talk to the owner, Conrad Thompson, and make him tell you about Johnny Mercer. Then get out of Georgia and go on up the South Carolina coast.

PLACES TO STAY IN THE SOUTHERN CORNER

BEAUFORT
Beaufort Inn
809 Port Republic Street
Beaufort 29902
(843) 521–9000

Craven Street Inn
1103 Craven Street
Beaufort 29902
(843) 522–1668

Cuthbert House Inn
1203 Bay Street
Beaufort 29902
(843) 521–1315

Port Republic Inn
915 Port Republic Street
Beaufort 29902
(843) 770–0600

PLACES TO EAT IN THE SOUTHERN CORNER

BEAUFORT
Rhett House Inn & Fine Dining
1009 Craven Street
Beaufort 29902
(843) 524–9030

EDISTO ISLAND
Old Post Office Restaurant
1442 Highway 174
Edisto Island 29438
(843) 869–2339

Pavilion Restaurant
102 Palmetto Boulevard
Edisto Island 29438
(843) 869–3061

RIDGELAND
Plantation Inn Restaurant
Highway 17
Ridgeland 29902
(843) 726–5510

ST. HELENA ISLAND
Gullah House Restaurant
859 Sea Island Parkway
St. Helena Island 29920

Shrimp Shack
1925 Sea Island Parkway
St. Helena Island 29920
(843) 838–2962

SAVANNAH, GEORGIA
Crystal Beer Parlor
301 West Jones Street
Savannah, GA 31401
(912) 232–1153

The Grand Strand

Fishing Villages and Wildlife Refuges

Along the coastline north of Charleston the land stays about the same as in the preceding areas for about 100 miles: sandy beaches, barrier islands, and thick swampland. Then around Surfside and northward the islands begin to thin out and a great wide beach, known as the Grand Strand, takes over and continues all the way to the North Carolina line.

Forty miles north of Charleston on Route 17, the tiny village of McClellanville has sat peacefully under the live oaks along Jeremy Creek for the past 200 years. This quaint little commercial fishing village came into national prominence in late September of 1989 when the full brunt of Hurricane Hugo hit here and destroyed or damaged every standing structure. At the height of the storm most of the citizens of McClellanville, who thought they were safe inside the brand-new Lincoln High School, were playing cards by flashlight, listening to their radios, and sleeping. Suddenly the storm punched out thirteen air-conditioner casements, and water cascaded down the halls and into the rooms. Inside the cafeteria/auditorium where 1,200 people were gathered, the water quickly reached the incredible height of 6 feet. To save themselves from drowning, the men, women, and children climbed up on desks, tables, and chairs and the small stage at the end of the big room. Many men and women, standing on chairs standing on tables, punched out ceiling panels and placed their children up on the thin metal support beams, where they stayed until the storm finally stopped around 3:00 in the morning.

One teacher in charge of a group of infants and some elderly people on the far side of the building thought she would spend the night high and dry in her small classroom. But when she looked outside through the glass-partitioned steel door, she almost had a heart attack. Before her very eyes, shrimp and fish were swimming by. The water outside the building had risen to more than 10 feet. Quickly she led her charges down the dark halls to the cafeteria only to face the unbelievable sight

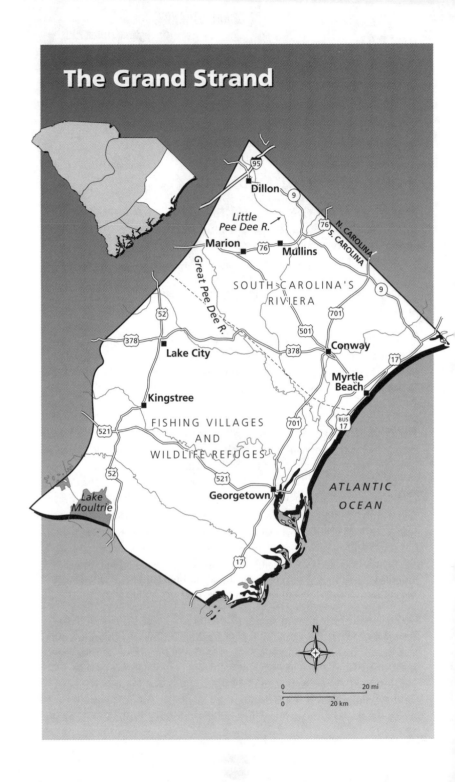

The Grand Strand

Dillon

95

9

Little
Pee Dee R.

76

N. CAROLINA
S. CAROLINA

Marion

76

Mullins

SOUTH CAROLINA'S
RIVIERA

9

Great Pee Dee R.

52

701

378

501

378

Conway

Lake City

17

Kingstree

Myrtle
Beach

521

FISHING VILLAGES
AND
WILDLIFE REFUGES

701

BUS
17

52

521

Lake
Moultrie

Georgetown

ATLANTIC
OCEAN

17

N

0   20 mi

0   20 km

AUTHOR'S FAVORITE PLACES

Laurel Hill Plantation
(Route 17 near
McClellanville)

Georgetown Ice Company
(Georgetown)

Brookgreen Gardens
(Route 17 at Murrells Inlet)

Yawkey Wildlife Center
(Route 17 near
Georgetown)

House of Blues
(Barefoot Landing, North
Myrtle Beach)

Tidewater Golf Course
(Little River)

of the fast-rising water. Miraculously the water stopped rising at 6 feet, 1 inch. Even more miraculously, no one was injured.

It took McClellanville more than five years to rebuild, but the marks that Hugo left behind will be here forever. At the Lincoln High School a bronze plaque at the entrance to the cafeteria shows where the water crested.

On Pinckney Street, the main street in McClellanville, stop at **The Country Store.** The owners and operators here are the affable and entertaining Buster Brown and his wife, Sherry. After Hugo blasted through town there was talk of turning the 110-year-old building into a convenience store, but the Browns stepped in, bought it, and rebuilt it to about what it was before the storm struck. Today they sell literally everything here, from groceries to fishing tackle, from fresh shrimp and fish to socks and T-shirts. They also serve a very fine breakfast, a lunch, and a fresh seafood or steak dinner. Prices are modest; dinners cost up to $12. Call (843) 877–3331.

You can loaf around here on the bench out front with a beer or a Blenheim Ginger Ale, a strong, stinging, head-clearing ginger ale produced up in Blenheim, South Carolina; some folks can't seem to live without it. The natives here will be happy to tell you what they were doing when Hugo came through and the shrimp and fish were swimming out on Route 17, more than 4 miles from the ocean.

Buster and Sherry can help you do nearly anything you'd want to do here. They can get you a room, a fishing pole, groceries, prescriptions, and much more. If you have a couple of kids and they want to go fishing, Buster and Sherry will sell, rent, or lend you a pole and all the gear you need. Then they'll sell you some bait and take you down to the inlet and show you exactly where the fish are biting.

McClellanville only has one bed-and-breakfast—**The Village Bed and Breakfast,** owned and operated by Cheri and Matthew George. This very quaint one-room unit is attached to the main house by a breezeway. During Hugo the entire place was floated completely off its foundation, but the Georges had it hauled back and everything was repaired. Matthew, along with being a first-class carpenter, is an artist who works in oils, watercolors, and prints. Much of his work is on display here and is modestly priced. Call ahead for reservations or for a look at his artwork. Call (843) 887–3266.

If you would like to see **Lincoln High School** and the high-water mark in bronze in the cafeteria, and maybe hear some more Hugo stories, turn left on Dupre to Lincoln Road. The school will be right in front of you. Most of the school's current faculty was here the night Hugo struck; everyone has a fascinating story.

The **McClellanville United Methodist Church** on the corner of Pinckney and Dupre is ideal for a photograph if you step back far enough and get a shot through the live oaks when the sun and shadows are right. Another block away is the brown-shingled **St. James Episcopal Church,** which is also surrounded by live oaks. The last time I was here at least a dozen mockingbirds were up in the trees. If you're from anywhere north of Yonkers and have trouble identifying mockingbirds, just look for the sergeant's stripes on their wings. You can also whistle a three-, four-, or five-note tune and, if you're lucky and they're in the right mood, they'll play it back for you.

Since there is only one B&B here in McClellanville, and it has only one room, you can also find lodgings at the nearby **Laurel Hill Plantation,** 8913 Highway 17 North, McClellanville, 29458. Go back out Pinckney Street to Route 17 and turn left. Drive 4.3 miles until you come to the fire station on the left. Cross over here and within 50 yards you will see the sign for Laurel Plantation. Pay attention to the sign that says 5 MPH WHEN WET, 15 MPH WHEN DRY. About a mile down this pleasant, winding, soft, sandy road you'll see a sight that comes right out of the movies— Laurel Plantation is surrounded by Spanish moss, draped live oaks, and looks out over an enormous and beautiful marsh. The stunning old mansion has six marvelous bed-and-breakfast rooms. Lee and Jackie Harrison own the place, and it's considered one of the finest in the state. On the big wraparound porch overlooking the marsh and the inlet, you'll find a 12-foot old-fashioned jogging board for the kids. The Morrisons also have a pontoon boat and delight in taking their guests out for a spin on the inlet and pointing out the spots of interest. Call (843) 887–3708 for prices and reservations.

Nearby is the tiny village of **Awendaw,** which was also leveled by Hugo. Oysters from here and nearby **Bull Bay** are famous all over South Carolina. The village owes much of its livelihood to their preparation for shipping.

Sewee Bay, a mile or so away, was named for an Indian tribe, and on its shores are numerous mounds of refuse and broken pottery from their prehistoric dwellings. After the white settlers came, the Sewee Indians felt that the English were not giving them a fair deal, so they planned to seek the English king and personally lay their grievances before him. Building huge canoes, they sailed into the open sea and were never heard of again. A pirate captured soon after the Indians' disappearance swore that he had seen the canoes far out in the Atlantic.

Not to be confused with the Sewee war party that struck out for England, the *Sewee Restaurant,* Route 17, Awendaw 29429, back down the road on Route 17 is probably the finest spot on the coastline for fresh seafood. The phone number is (843) 928–3609 and the hours are from 11:00 A.M. to 9:00 P.M. Monday through Thursday and 11:00 A.M. to 10:00 P.M. Friday, 8:00 A.M. to 10:00 P.M. Satuday, and 11:00 A.M. to 3:00 P.M. Sunday. Prices for lunch start at $8.95 and go up to $18.95. The delicious dinners range from $8.95 to $19.95. Since Sewee is only a few miles from McClellanville they get all of their shrimp, soft-shell crabs, and flounder right off the boat. In other words, this is fresh seafood that really means fresh. You might even enjoy going to the McClellanville docks, watching the boats come in, and then taking the pleasant ride back through the old fishing town that Hugo almost destroyed but is now back up to speed.

Still on Route 17, a couple hundred yards south of the McClellanville turnoff, you can stop at the *Crab Pot* for a very fine lunch or dinner. This airy, friendly spot right on the highway serves an excellent shrimp salad as well as hamburgers for lunch and a full menu for dinner. Prices range from $5.00 to $8.00 for lunch and up to $14.00 for dinner. Call (843) 887–3156.

Close by on Route 17—you'll have to watch for the signs—is *The Hampton Plantation.* Set back from the road on a 2.5-mile drive, this is one of the finest examples of antebellum architecture in the entire South. When Henry Middleton Rutledge departed Hampton to serve the Confederacy during the Civil War, he left behind one of the grandest homes and most prosperous agricultural enterprises in America. The decades before the Civil War witnessed the high point of rice cultivation in South Carolina, and Hampton Plantation was one of the leaders. At this time Hampton was using the daily action of the tides on the freshwater rivers to irrigate the fields.

When Colonel Rutledge returned to Hampton Plantation in 1865, he returned to an entirely different South, one in which Hampton Plantation would never again hold the position it once had as a center of political and economic life in the state. The grand house remained unpainted and in decay; cotton was stored in the grand ballroom; crops were planted among the live oaks on the once stately lawn. By 1923 both the Colonel and his wife were dead, and the house stood abandoned.

The Colonel's son, Archibald Hamilton Rutledge—outdoorsman, writer, and the first poet laureate of South Carolina—returned to Hampton from teaching school in Pennsylvania and at age fifty-six began a long process of renovating the mansion. He described his labor of love in his best-known book, *Home by the River*: "When I first came back, it was sagging in places and it had not been painted in a generation. Now everything has been done to restore it without changing it and it gleams under its four coats of white paint. It is no unusual thing for visitors to tell me that in its simple dignity it is the most impressive home they have ever seen."

Now protected under the auspices of **Hampton Plantation State Park,** 1950 Rutledge Road, McClellanville 29458, the mansion may be opened by appointment or rented for special occasions. A nominal fee ($2.00) is charged for admission to the mansion. A guided tour of the house, the grounds, and the nature trails surrounding the mansion can be arranged by calling (843) 546–9361. The park itself is open daily year-round from 9:00 A.M. to 6:00 P.M. The mansion is open year-round Thursday to Monday from 1:00 to 4:00 P.M. It is closed Tuesday and Wednesday. There is also a tour boat that carries you out to nearby Bull Island. Times and fares are available on request.

While this plantation is truly one of the great sights of this part of the country, the unsuspecting traveler must be warned of a little item down here that can cause considerable discomfort—the deer fly. This noxious little beast can reduce a full-grown man or woman to quivering suet in minutes. Be prepared by picking up an insect repellent from Buster Brown back in McClellanville. Long-sleeved shirts are also advised. Travel tip: The deer fly is not confined to the Hampton Estates—it is literally everywhere down here. Also available are the no-see-ums and gnats. In any case, an insect repellent and long-sleeved shirts will solve what could be a terrible problem.

A friend of mine interviewed a 110-year-old gentleman not too long ago and posed the question of what was the most important single invention he had witnessed in the century behind him. The old man counted on his fingers: the automobile, the airplane, the atomic bomb, landing on the moon, and the computer. Then he said, "Now these are all very fine, but you know something, if I've got to go with the one that's the most important for me, I've got to go with screens."

On up Route 17, a mile and a half north of Georgetown, turn off at the sign for **Hobcaw Barony** (843) 546–4623 and go to the **Kimbel Lodge** at the right of the gate, at 22 Hobcaw Road, Georgetown 29440. Here you can collect enough wildlife information to last a lifetime. A sample of the free seminars are "South Carolina Butterflies and How to Attract Them," and "Voices of Spring: What's Happening to Our Migratory Songbirds?"

Wildlife trips include "The Interesting World of Oysters." The course blurb reads, "Live marine critters will be collected and viewed with microscopes at the Baruch Marine Lab. Participants will also learn how to safely harvest these razor-sharp bivalves. We'll even steam some for those who still have an appetite for oysters after studying the creatures that live in and around them. Wear old clothes and bring gloves and boots for walking in the mud."

This four-hour tour is limited to twenty people; the fee is $10. Other tours originating from Kimbel Lodge are "The Fishes of North Inlet Estuary," "Songbird Banding Workshop," and "Birds of Punkinseed Island."

The modern history of Hobcaw Barony began at the turn of the century. In the winter of 1905 Bernard Baruch acquired all of the land that once made up ten rice plantations. Hobcaw's tranquil woods and waters provided Baruch with recreation and relief from the pressures of public life. Mr. Baruch shared the peaceful world of Hobcaw with his family, friends, and many distinguished associates, including Sir Winston Churchill and President Franklin Delano Roosevelt. In the old mansion you can see photographs of Baruch on various hunting trips as well as shots of him with Churchill and Roosevelt. The barony includes about 9,000 acres of tidal wetlands, oyster reefs, former rice fields, and waterways on or bordering the Belle W. Baruch Foundation's 17,500-acre wildlife refuge.

The Kimbel Lodge at the entrance to the estate has wonderful exhibits of Low Country animals and plants. The kids will be especially delighted with the live baby alligator, but for goodness' sake, don't touch it!

If you're hungry and heading north on Route 17, watch on the left side of the road for the sign **Hog Heaven.** There's no address here, but if you miss it you can make a U-turn and go back. The old owner, George Young, used to say that "Some people on the road smell the smoke and make the turn and come back."

Hog Heaven, formerly Yum's Barbeque, has the finest pork barbecue on the eastern seaboard. Call (843) 237–PIGG. Hours are 11:00 A.M. to 8:00 P.M. Friday–Saturday. Prices range form $4.50 to $7.00.

Route 17 runs right through the heart of **Georgetown.** This is the third oldest city in South Carolina and is named after King George II. The entire district, which lies along the Sampit River and the white settlement of which dates back to the 1700s, is listed on the National Register of Historic Places. Long before the Revolutionary War most of the wealth of the town came from indigo; later it came from rice. Today the two main industries are steel and paper production, but the old, deep harbor is still an important shipping port.

The **Red Store Warehouse** (very early eighteenth century) is a good spot to start your tour of this fascinating town. Originally this was part of a three-story brick tavern that also stored silks, indigo, and imported wines, as well as mail from English ships. The glamorous Theodosia Burr Allston, daughter of Aaron Burr, sailed from this wharf in 1812

On Barbecue

When you arrive in the Palmetto State, you are in the official Tigris and Euphrates land of barbecue. Right down in here is where it all began. You have probably heard how Texas claims they have the best. Well, we shall now put that myth to rest. The Lone Star State, while it may have many wonderful things, does not have hickory wood. Without hickory wood you cannot have true barbecue. Now they may call what they serve barbecue, because it's a free country and they can call anything they cook, serve, and eat anything they want. But around here, if you mention Texas barbecue someone's going to drift out to the parking lot and check your license plates.

Down here in the "hard lard belt," our barbecue is cooked with hickory wood and hickory wood only, and the sauce is either mustard based or vinegar and pepper based. And that is the long and the short of it. North Carolina has hickory wood, and they have on occasion been known to produce a good three rib down cross-

breed hog. But your basic North Carolinian does not have good sense, because they will drench down that pork with ketchup-based sauce and that will not do it.

As far as I'm concerned—and I have been a judge on many barbecue contests and do not treat it lightly—South Carolina barbecue is, and always has been, light years ahead of the rest of the country. Using smaller hogs—the three ribs down category—and hickory wood and hickory coals, our barbecue will cross the finish line as tender as pound cake, and with our sauces and light bread and cole slaw and cold beer or lemonade, it will drop you to your knees, where you will weep tears of appreciation and never ending gratitude. At the Springfield Frog Jump, The Irmo Okra Strut, and the Salley "Chitlin Strut," I have seen serious men in business suits and full-grown Christian women go into what is called a "barbecue coma." So much for barbecue.

and was never seen again. Her husband, the governor of South Carolina, died of grief, or so the story goes.

Harborwalk is a 1,000-foot-long, 12-foot-wide boardwalk at the edge of the Sampit River. Along this walk are the back-door entrances and pastel awnings of the Front Street shops and restaurants. This is a delightful place to stroll and get your bearings. Three of the restaurants on Front Street look out over the boardwalk and water. The *River Room* at 801 Front, Georgetown 29440, is known for its excellent seafood salads, homemade french-fried onion rings, and its iced tea served in wide-mouthed Mason jars. Prices are from $6.00 to $12.00 for lunch. Dinner prices range from $6.00 to $19.95. Call (843) 527–4110.

Also on Front Street—you can't miss it—is the *Town Clock/Old Market* at 633 Front Street, Georgetown 29440. Call (843) 546–7423. Built in 1835, this tower was used as a marketplace, city hall, and lockup. Today it houses the *Rice Museum* on the second floor. It displays the history of the rice empire that flourished here in the nineteenth century. Admission is $2.00 for seniors, $3.00 for adults, $1.00 for students ages twelve to twenty-one, and free for children under twelve who are accompanied by an adult. Call (843) 546–7423.

Across the street is the Georgetown Chamber of Commerce at 10010 Front Street. Call (843) 546–8436. This is also a good spot to start a tour of the older sections of town. Here you can get maps, tourist information, schedules, and a list of bed-and-breakfasts in the area.

Be sure to pick up a Georgetown National Register Historic District Map. Since there are forty-four historic sites all within a comfortable walking distance, I'd suggest simply starting off from the Chamber with the map in your hand and following the numbers. Some truly delightful houses are on this walking tour.

A typical house on the tour is *Harold Kaminski House* at 1003 Front Street, Georgetown 29440. Call (843) 546–7706. Among those who lived here was Captain Dagget, a local hero who built the mine that sank the Union flagship *Harvest Moon* in Winyah Bay in 1865. Today the house has an outstanding collection of antiques from various periods.

The Georgetown Ice Company, 300 North Fraser Street, Georgetown 29440, a low, rambling filling station that has, over the years, turned into the biggest convenience store in the state, is a one-of-a-kind South Carolina wonder. Drop by for a cola or a Blenheim Ginger Ale. This store caters to fishermen, hunters, and anyone and everyone passing through. They sell everything, and you'll be hard pressed to name something they don't have. The range is incredible: fishing rods, tackle, worms, crickets, minnows, hot dogs, clothing, magazines, gas, oil, groceries, pharmaceuticals, boiled peanuts, et cetera, et cetera, et cetera. If you're from the north country, give boiled peanuts a chance. They'll seem vile at first, but they will definitely grow on you. Every time I go to New York City my friends there beg me to bring them a few large sacks. Call (843) 546–6169 if you want to, but there's no need to phone: They are open twenty-four hours a day, seven days a week.

The best bet for rooms downtown is at **Carolinian Inn** at 706 Church Street, Georgetown 29940. The rooms are pleasant and beautifully kept, and connecting rooms for when you're traveling with kids are available. The outdoor pool is surrounded by palm trees and a brick wall that keeps the breezes down, meaning you can swim almost any time. Continental breakfast is complimentary. Rates vary from $50 to $80. Call (843) 546–5191.

Directly across the street is the **Lafayette Restaurant,** 532 Church Street, Georgetown 29440, open six days a week from 5:00 A.M. to 10:00 P.M. This is a very, very popular spot for breakfast, among fishermen in particular. Try it. They have a way of serving you your eggs and bacon and grits and toast all at the same time. In other words, the toast is not getting cold while the rest of the meal is coming. The coffee is great; so are the waitresses. Go there and when you get back home spread the word that this is the place for the perfect breakfast. Call (843) 546–5033.

Blackwater Adventures is headed by Louis Nexus, a native with more than twenty years' experience in guiding people through the rivers and inlets in this area. Louis is strongly behind preserving and promoting the natural environment of South Carolina. He offers a trip called the **Low Country Sampler,** a six- to- seven-hour canoe trip that includes lunch and a choice of skeet shooting or freshwater fishing. The trip costs $65 for adults and is free for children age twelve and under. Another trip, the **Pinopolis Dam Lock System Tour,** allows you to see the largest single-step dam lock in the world, with a drop of 75 feet. Through the Santee Cooper Lake System (which were the largest artificial lakes in the world until the Aswan Dam was completed) this guided canoe trip provides some unforgettable scenery. Other exclusive trips and overnights in the area can be made by arrangement. Group discounts are also available. Call (800) 761–1850 for inquiries and reservations. Write them at P.O. Box 4639, Pinopolis 29469.

Carolina Safari is as eclectic as its tour director, Virgil Graham, who is an area native, a naturalist, and a magazine photographer. The mailing address is Carolina Safari, P.O. Box 6799, Myrtle Beach 29577. On the jeep tours of various sites in the Low Country, you will see egrets, bald eagles, alligators, maritime fossils, and a variety of ecosystems, including saltwater marshes, cypress swamps, and more. Narrative background on Indian, colonial, and antebellum history is offered along with examples of 300-year-old plantations, Drunken Jack's Island, and visits to other legendary haunts of the Low Country.

The jeeps are genuine, customized safari-style touring vehicles that seat ten to twelve people, and each one has a driver/guide. Binoculars are provided, stops are frequent and spontaneous, and you can take photos from any seat. Three-hour tours are offered daily at a cost of $30 for adults and $15 for children under age twelve. Pickup is available at most resorts and condos. Special tours and group rates can be arranged. Call (843) 497–5330 for reservations and further information.

Andrews Old Town Hall Museum, 14 West Main Street, Andrews 29510, is open Tuesday and Thursday only, from 10:00 A.M. until 4:00 P.M. or by appointment. The museum is located in the town of Andrew, inland 18 miles west of Georgetown on Route 521. Representing a typical Victorian-era Andrews home, everything in the museum is circa 1909, the year Andrews was founded. Included are a child's room with period toys, a complete kitchen, and a Victorian parlor with period furniture, pictures, a pump organ, and a Victrola. Also depicting 1909 life are a complete Victorian schoolroom and a farm shed with tools, scales, harnesses and traces, hogshead containers, a plow, and plow points. Call (843) 264–3471.

North of Georgetown a few miles, you're in *Pawleys Island* country. The bumper stickers on the cars of some of the summer inhabitants say ARROGANTLY SHABBY. Despite this cloying little observation, the people are friendly and the island is a one-of-a-kind gem. Many of the beach houses have been here since long before the Civil War.

Just staying on Pawleys Island for a week or so is in itself a perfect vacation, but there is much more to do here than just bake in the sun and watch for porpoises. Take fishing, specifically surf fishing. You need no license, and you can fish literally anywhere on the beach where you can cast a line. Surf fishing starts in the spring and the favorite spots are right here: the south end of Litchfield Beach, the south and north end of Pawleys, and the south end of Garden City Beach. All of these run together, so there's no trouble finding your way. For surf fishing you'll need a surf rod, which you can buy or rent from almost any store in Pawleys. The rod should be between 8 and 11 feet long with an open-face saltwater reel, filled with 10- to 20-pound test monofilament line. You should also have two or three bottom-rig end tackles with three-ounce pyramid sinkers and 2/0 hooks. You'll need a sand spike to hold your rod, some fresh mullet cut in 1-inch pieces, sunglasses, a cooler filled with your favorite drinks, a beach towel or chair to sit on, and a good book to read.

Why the book? In the spring, three major species of fish are in the surf: sea trout, red drum that have moved out of the estuaries, and bluefish that are moving north along the coast. If any of these fish happen to be feeding, you can get all kinds of action. If the fish haven't arrived at your spot on the beach or have just passed by, you'll have plenty of time to read.

No one really knows what happens when you're sitting in a beach chair with your feet in the water and a surf rod sticking in a sand spike, but it seems that life definitely slows down and down and down. Up and down the endless beach you'll see the young and the old, the fat and the slim doing it all day, every day. But it's not all just sitting there. Every half hour or so you can rise up, crank in the line, and then cast it out again. Then you can sit back down.

If you enjoy this kind of serenity, stop at the **Pawleys Island Supplies,** 10460 Ocean Highway, Pawleys Island 29585 (843–237–2912) on Route 17, rent some equipment, and come on down.

If surf fishing and surf sitting aren't dramatic enough for you, you can charter a boat at Georgetown and head out for the Gulf Stream 60 miles away and try your luck with white marlin, blue marlin, dolphin, wahoo, or yellowfin tuna. All fishing tackle and bait are furnished, and you'll have a skilled but expensive captain with radar equipment for spotting the fish and getting you there. The bad news on the price is that it can run as high as $1,200 for the day and you need at least a week for reservations. The good news is that you can take along five buddies, which comes out to $200 each.

While you're out in the Gulf Stream, the temperature will be hotter (more than 100 degrees), the water will be greener, and you'll see clumps of fern and kelp and whole stalks of coconut trees drifting by from as far away as Barbados. You might fish all day and not get a single strike. But then again you might hook into an 800-pound tarpon or a 400-pound sailfish or find yourself plowing through a school of 200-pound amberjack.

Brookgreen Gardens, a former indigo and rice plantation, is an outdoor sculpture garden, located on Route 17 at Murrells Inlet 29576. Call (843) 237–4218. It was originally purchased by the Henry Huntington family as a setting for their art collection. It is now acclaimed as the world's finest collection of American figurative sculpture. If you like the work of Remington, you'll like this. One particular piece will please the kids: a life-size sculpture of an alligator by David Turner. The current total number of pieces in the collection is 547 works by 241 artists; the collection is still growing. At the

Brookgreen Gardens, Murrells Inlet

entrance is the famous *Fighting Stallions* by Anna Hyatt Huntington; it is the largest sculpture ever cast in aluminum.

This entire garden, with its incredible expanse of grass and beautiful landscape and wildlife, is well worth the visit. While here you will also get an idea of how a plantation should look. The 9,127 acres of Brookgreen Gardens extend from the beachfront on the Atlantic Ocean to the freshwater swamps along the Waccamaw River. The garden's paths are laid out in the shape of a butterfly, and flowers bloom here from early spring right into September. The Terrace Cafe on the grounds overlooks a truly wonderful view of the park and the woods; it serves sandwiches, salads, soups, and snacks. Picnic facilities are located opposite the sculpture gardens' parking lot, next to Jessamine Park. This is the perfect spot for a picnic and is a delightful place to spend several hours. Once again, pack your favorite insect repellent and be prepared for deer flies and no-see-ums. A gift shop here offers gifts, books, and items that tell the story of Brookgreen Gardens. Admission here is $8.50 for adults, $4.00 for children ages six to twelve, and free for children age five and younger. Open daily from 9:30 A.M. to 5:00 P.M. Call (843) 237–4218.

Belle Isle and **Battery White** originally belonged to Revolutionary hero Peter Horry, for whom Horry County is named. Battery White, an earthen Confederate fortification, was built on the plantation overlooking the bay for the defense of Georgetown during the Civil War. A short distance offshore here lies the sunken Union flagship *Harvest Moon,* which went down during the last days of Georgetown's Union occupation when a Confederate bomb planted on board went off. The entrance to Belle Isle, now a resort community, is located south of Georgetown on South Island Road off Route 17. There is no charge to visit Battery White. For access, go to the Belle Isle guard gate, which is clearly marked on Route 17.

Due to the popularity of the *Yawkey Wildlife Center* tour, located at 1 Yawkey Way South, Georgetown 29440, reservations here must be made three to six months in advance. Call (843) 546–6814. Accessible only by boat, the Yawkey preserve consists of North and South Island and most of Cat Island, three coastal islands at the mouth of Winyah Bay. Willed to the state wildlife department by the late Tom Yawkey, who owned the Boston Red Sox, the center is dedicated to the management of waterfowl habitat. In cooperation with other state agencies, this center was largely responsible for saving the brown pelican a few years back. Today these birds are no longer on the endangered species list. As a matter of fact, if you're on almost any of the islands down here, you can count as many as fifty or sixty brown pelicans in a single formation as they fly home in the evening.

The Hammock Shop, 10880 Ocean Highway at Pawley's Island 29585, is open year-round, Monday through Saturday from 10:00 A.M. to 6:00 P.M. and Sunday from 1:00 to 5:00 P.M., except summer hours are 9:30 A.M. to 8:00 P.M. from mid-June through August. Since 1938 this has been a favorite destination down here in the Low Country for shoppers. Originally set up to make and sell rope hammocks, they now sell cookbooks, clothing, and beachwear, as well as another hundred items to take home as gifts. One of their most popular items is their famous rope hammocks, which you can see being made right before your eyes. If you want solid comfort and absolutely no danger of falling out, get the wider version, which can accommodate two people.

The Hammock Shop's charming *Tyler's Cove* restaurant specializes in fresh seafood and Low Country cuisine. It also offers weekly specials and a raw/steamed seafood bar. At *Sweet Temptations* you can get homemade candies, cookies, taffy, and pastries as well as delicious soups, salads, and deli sandwiches. Be sure to stop at the *Pawleys Island Ice Cream Shop,* too. Finally, *The Hammock Shop General Store* is truly a wonderful and imaginative gift store featuring a large collection of South Carolina books, recipes, and local ghost stories as well as best-sellers. If you want to take a gift to the folks back home, this is probably the best spot to shop on the coast.

Pawleys Island and Litchfield Beaches became, in a real sense, the first resort in America. Some say that since they were separated from the mainland by large salt marshes, malaria-bearing mosquitoes could not fly across them. Pawleys Island in particular became a favorite refuge for wealthy planter families, some of whose houses are still standing today. These planters also built large and lavish houses in Charleston and stayed there during the "social season" of February, which was after the crops were harvested. All the romantic images so often associated with the "Old South" and *Gone with the Wind* grew out of this period.

If you'd like to stay overnight here, and who wouldn't, stop by **Pawleys Island Business Association** on Route 17 at The Planter's Exchange. They'll show you a wide range of places to stay, including a 200-year-old beach house, a plantation manor house, bed-and-breakfasts, ocean-front hotel rooms and suites, and rooms and houses on the beach, on the creek, or on one of the many golf courses.

If you ignore the Route 17 bypass and stay on old Route 17, you'll go right through the heart of Murrells Inlet. Founded in the late eighteenth

Recipe for Corn Whiskey

*T*hese are the facts: (1)it's legal to make it; (2) it's illegal to sell it; (3) if it's made wrong, it will kill you.

Ingredients and equipment:
50 lbs of corn meal
100 lbs of sugar
One thick horse blanket
An old-fashioned hand-cranked clothes wringer

First we mix our meal and sugar in a fifty-gallon pot and pour in enough boiling water to fill it. Cover it for three days and nights or until it begins to "work." In the winter you may need an extra day. You then cook the mix—it is now called "mash." As it begins to cook, cover the pot with the horse blanket. After a half hour or so—depending on how hot you have your fire—the blanket will begin to sag with the steam. You then remove it and run it though the clothes wringer. What you see coming out is corn whiskey. It's not great corn whiskey, but it's corn whiskey nevertheless. It's also the perfect way a layman can understand the process. All whiskey stills operate on this basis. Every still—whether here in the Carolina pines or over in Scotland at the House of Johnny Walker—follows this same basic practice—mix their mash, cook it, catch the steam, and condense it. The rest is aging and advertising. Any questions?

century by Captain Murrell, Murrells Inlet has supplied the Waccamaw Neck area with fresh seafood for over 200 years. Fleets of deep-sea fishing boats lie at anchor here and journey daily out to the Gulf Stream to bring back every possible kind of fish for the local restaurants.

Just off Murrells Inlet lies Drunken Jack's Island, where, according to local legend, a pirate named Jack was accidentally marooned with no provisions except his shipmate's excess rum supply. Months later, when the ship returned to load up the rum cargo, all the crew found was case after empty case and spent rum bottles all along the shore, plus the bleached bones of poor Jack. The treasure of Blackbeard is also reputed to be buried here.

The highway meanders along under ancient live oaks by many unique seafood restaurants, ranging from old, weathered, time-honored culinary jewels with third-generation chefs and proprietors to more recent dining establishments with troubadours to delight the evening diners.

Perhaps the oldest and best known dining spot is *Oliver's Lodge,* 4204 Route 17, Murrells Inlet 29576, where they have been serving fresh fish, shrimp, and ribs since 1910. Everyone I know keeps going back and going back. When you go insist on a table on the back porch overlooking the view of the inlet. Dinners range from $15 to $25. Open seven days a week. Call for reservations at (843) 651–2963.

Inlet House Café is open daily from 6:00 A.M. to 2:00 P.M. Call (843) 651–0622 for reservations. This popular spot, owned and operated by Lee Sanders, features traditional Low Country seafood.

Nance's Creek Front Restaurant, Highway 17, Murrells Inlet 29576, has a dining room with at least 100 feet of glass looking out over the marsh and the creek. The view is spectacular because you can see the boats coming in and going out and watch the changing colors on the marsh grass. The food is almost as good as the view. Prices are from $16 to $30. Open Monday through Saturday, 4:00–10:00 P.M., and 4:00–9:00 P.M. Sunday. Call (843) 651–2696.

Murrells Inlet is the absolute center for fishing down here. You can fish for almost anything you can imagine. As a matter of fact, the South Carolina coastline and creeks and inland lakes probably offer a larger variety of fish than any place in the country. The only problem fish are the sharks and stingrays. Swimmers are warned to avoid large schools of fish, for the sharks feed among them. One sign of a shark feeding among fish is the presence of birds, which are waiting to scavenge the scraps.

The stingray is a bottom-dweller in the ocean and salt marshes. It won't attack, but its tail has a clever little barb that can cause a painful wound if it's stepped on. You are cautioned to shuffle your feet when wading in the water, so that they sense you coming and get out of your way. Be on the lookout for jellyfish and man-of-wars. If they sting you, a quick remedy is to sprinkle the irritated area with meat tenderizer.

Along with charter-boat fishing for sport fish, there are two other types of fishing, namely, party-boat fishing and pier fishing. On the party boat you will certainly catch fish, but be prepared to put up with a few problems. Beer is sold on board, and, in the hot sun and after a night on the town, a few of your shipmates will be hooked over the rail doing you know what. To avoid having this happen to you, be sure to eat a very light and very dry breakfast. In other words, leave the grease alone. The trip is long—six hours. Once the big boat and its typically hundred-plus passengers leave the pier there is no turning back. None, no matter what. On the other hand, it's cheap—$15 to $20 for six hours with rod and reel and bait all thrown in. If you can stand the heat, the captain, who knows the waters and the ways of the fish, will take you places where you can catch something. Children often have a better time here than adults.

If you don't want to get on board a party boat, the pier a couple miles north at Surfside is the easiest fishing in the world—and very pleasant. Here you can rent a rod and reel and buy bait and walk out on the half-mile pier to any seat you like. You cast your line in and sit back and enjoy the breeze. Pier fishers tend to be very agreeable people and will be pleased to answer any questions you have about bait and casting, and they may even identify what you might catch. Since most of the pier is lighted, many fishermen come carrying chaise lounges, blankets, coolers

Fishing: The Party Boat

*O*f all of the sport-fishing boats that smoke out of Murrells Inlet heading for the Gulf Stream sixty miles out in search of marlin, tuna, and the great white shark, the bottom of the line is the party boat. This is a big iron monster that resembles a locomotive and stretches out 80 to 90 feet, with metal tubes every 18 inches for holding your rods. Standing side by side with another 130 customers, you get the feeling that you are chained together on a slave ship bound for some Dutch possession. Leaving the harbor, the boat throws up a wake so big other fishermen scream and shake their fists. But despite the crowd, and the perfunctory way you are treated, the party boat is the only fishing that posts the sign:

WE GUARANTEE—YOU WILL CATCH FISH! OR YOUR MONEY BACK!

of food, and radios and stay all night. For regular daytime fishing you might catch anything from a blowfish to a shark. With a little luck, you can catch almost anything here if you're patient enough and the weather is right. Try to fish when the tide is coming in, not going out. When it's incoming, the fish follow it in to feed. The only problem you'll have out here if the fish are biting is that the kids will never want to come in.

Surfside Pier, just north of Murrells Inlet, is, at 800 feet, one of the longest fishing piers in the state. It's open twenty-four hours a day, seven days a week, and is lighted for night fishing. Prices are in the ballpark; $6.00 to rent a rod and reel, $6.00 to fish, and $3.00 for bait. Call the Surfside Pier at (843) 238–0121. Out on the end of the pier many people fish with big rods and reels and often land spectacular catches. The record down here is a 128-pound tarpon that one George Singleton caught out on the end; he wore out a pair of shoes fighting the fish all the way back to the shore.

Surfside Pier is full of surprise catches. You'll see sand sharks, hammerheads, blowfish, and often a sheepshead the size of a good-sized Labrador retriever. Down the middle of the pier are benches, and the old-timers staked out here are usually natives who can and will give you any information you want about the winds and the tides. They'll also be able to identify the strange creatures drawn up from the bottom. The sea robin is of particular interest—it has wings like a bat and a face like a catfish.

Almost everyone likes to talk and give advice down here. Take advantage of it. Take a long walk out to the end of the pier and ask anybody anything you want about fishing. It's amazing how much they know and how much there is to know. They will also tell you exactly what line, bait, and hook to use and exactly where to throw it in.

The Surfside Pier tackle shop has cold drinks, crackers, and so on, but for a very good meal at a fair price try *Nibil's,* right on the pier at 11 South Ocean Boulevard, Surfside 29575. The view up and down the beach and out over the Atlantic is especially nice in the mornings and evenings. Nibil's is open from 6:30 A.M. to 9:00 P.M. Monday through Saturday. Breakfast and lunch only are served on Sunday. The most popular breakfast is their country ham, grits, and eggs. Dinners range from $6.00 to $20.00; the specialties are fresh flounder, snapper, scallops, and Angus beef. The manager is Jack Cahill. He's outgoing and easy to talk to and knows just about everything there is to know about Surfside and the surrounding area. Call (843) 238–5080.

For fishing from the beach, all you need is a rod and reel, a chair, an umbrella, and a book to read. For bait use shrimp or squid or section up a small perch. Don't forget to bring along a hollow stake to hold up the pole.

South Carolina's Riviera

Ten miles north of Surfside you'll come to the outskirts of Myrtle Beach, an oasis that has been called everything from The Redneck Riviera to Blue Collar Mecca to Golfer's Heaven. Each of these descriptions fits like a glove. In February and March the Canadians swarm over the place, swim in the ocean, eat the all-you-can-eat breakfasts of pancakes, eggs, and bacon, and play eighteen holes in the morning and eighteen more in the afternoon. Most of them drive down. So if you see four men or four women wearing golf caps with the car trunk riding low with golf clubs and the roof rack piled high with golfing paraphernalia, they're heading for Myrtle Beach and they're harmless. To celebrate their arrival, the Myrtle Beach Chamber of Commerce floods the streets with Canadian flags, street-wide Canadian banners, and Canadian everything.

Figuring each golf course down here is approximately 5½ miles long and the South Carolina coastline has more than one hundred courses, the mathematics tell us that if you laid them end to end they would extend all the way from Little River, the northernmost point in South Carolina, across all of the Georgia coastline, and more than 200 miles into Florida. In other words, there are a lot of courses down here.

Cooking Fish

You scale it, clean it, load it down with cracker crumbs, and lay it gently in 550-degree grease. You turn it once. Only once. The fish is done when it looks done. On fried fish, which is the best fish, down here we eat everything—the tail, the dorsal fin, the mouth, head, eyes and all. The cats, returning to some ancient savagery, dispose of the darker organs, then calm down to clean and polish the bones. And since any walking hound prefers fish bones to pork chop and chicken bones, the rest goes out on the step for Old Trailer and his youngest son, Boomer. In short, the cooking of fish, like of the hog and the Great Plains buffalo, is ecologically perfect; there is no waste. Fish scales are scalloped around the "God Bless Our Mortgaged Home" signs and, in the hands of an inspired artist, gilded gold and blue and magenta to liven up the seashell memorabilia that crowd the mantels from Cocoa Beach to the Outer Banks along the North Carolina coast.

Road Signs to Watch For

On Route 17: WELCOME TO NORTH MYRTLE BEACH, THE HOME OF VANNA WHITE.

Near Andrews: WELCOME TO ANDREWS, HOME OF CHUBBY CHECKER.

Golf is just one of the attractions here. Myrtle Beach sits on the very center of the Grand Strand, a 60-mile stretch of pristine beach that is uninterrupted by tidal inlets. Much of the beach slopes gently into the water and is ideal for kids, even small ones. Campers from everywhere are welcome here; the area provides more than 12,000 campsites. The Grand Strand is also the yearly after-graduation destination for thousands of high school kids who arrive every June for a week of beach music, walking up and down the promenade, hanging out at the Pavilion, and wide-open revelry.

Finally, Myrtle Beach has become a popular retirement spot for northerners who like the weather, the beach, the golf, the food, and the general laid-back attitude. Adding all these visitors together at the height of the season, the population soars to more than 350,000. But, despite the crush and heavy commercialization, you'll find nice touches of the Old South and friendly faces everywhere.

Outlet Park at 3071 Waccamaw Boulevard, Myrtle Beach 29577, Waccamaw (843–236–6221) is open daily year-round. To find it take the Route 17 bypass to Route 501 to the Intracoastal Waterway between Conway and Myrtle Beach. If you can't find it, just follow the cars—everyone is going there. The place is so big and spread out it reminds me of the Atlanta airport. With more than one hundred stores it has enough variety for any kind of shopper. Along with luggage, clothes, shoes, sheets, and pillowcases, you can even get a light meal here as well as a beer. You can eat at an outdoor table and watch the bewildered shoppers schlepping along, buying everything they can carry. The place is so big they have shuttles from one mall to the next.

Ten miles north of Myrtle Beach on property now owned by the Myrtle Beach Hilton is *Arcadian Shores Golf Club.* This course, designed by Reis Jones, one of the premier golf architects on the scene today, combines the best of Mother Nature and the best of a modern golf course layout. The 13th and 14th holes, the signature holes, cross a cypress-studded lake that looks as if it's been here since the beginning of time. The tall pines, magnolias, and live oaks that frame the rest of the course create the perfect setting for the layout, which *Golf Magazine* and *Golf Digest* have placed in their top fifty year in and year out.

Since the purchase by the Hilton chain, guests here at the hotel have been granted preferential tee times, but the course is open year-round to guests staying in a number of other select hotels in the Myrtle Beach

More Golf Advice

*P*ro-Fit Inc., owned and operated by Mike Harris at 1616 Highway 17 South in North Myrtle Beach, phone number (843) 361–0102, is a must stop for all serious golfers. Mike, a genuine wizard with every aspect of golf, has an amazing discovery that you must try out. For no charge he will test your clubs on a frequency vibration machine. There is a strong chance even the best and most expensive club shafts aren't matched properly. Mike will show you which ones are not in sync with the others, then he'll match it with rest of the clubs and sell you what you need at a very moderate price. When all your clubs have the same frequency, only then are they truly matched, and only then can you swing with the same swing. While this is no guarantee to bring your handicap down, it will do wonders for your confidence, which after all is what the golf swing is all about. It works for me.

area. Arcadian Shores has recently been overhauled and improved. Under the Hilton management it has never been in better shape. For a weekend of top-flight golf, with a guaranteed tee time, only a few hundred yards from the Hilton, you'll have to go a long way to beat Arcadian Shores. While staying at the Hilton, by the way, you can play almost any one of the sixty-odd courses within 30 miles of here. For information write to Arcadian Shores Golf Club, 701 Hilton Road, Myrtle Beach 29572, or call (843) 449–5217.

Back down Route 17 you'll see signs for **The Dunes Golf and Beach Club.** This is the site of the annual Golf Writers of America Clambake, which is held every year one week before The Masters. Robert Trent Jones designed the holes in such a way that the wind hits golfers from every direction on the compass. What he has done is lived up to the old Scottish saying, "No wind, no golf."

The club and clubhouse are right on the ocean, with a beautiful view of the beach. The Dunes, probably the most famous course on the beach, is a must for golfing in South Carolina. Last year they hosted the U.S. Seniors Open. While the club is private, guests staying at a number of select hotels on the beach are allowed to play. So when you're making reservations, the first question you ask should not concern the rates, or if the room is on the ocean, or whether the bed comes equipped with Magic Fingers, but whether the hotel guarantees that you can play The Dunes. If it doesn't, tell them you'll call back. Then call the desk at The Dunes and ask them where you should stay. Call (843) 449–5236 or write The Dunes Golf and Beach Club, 9000 North Ocean Boulevard, Myrtle Beach 29572.

Both The Dunes and Arcadian Shores abound with deer and raccoons. The rare fox squirrel—bigger than a regular squirrel and with a black mask around its eyes—is sometimes seen here. Watch for it. You might also see pileated woodpeckers, alligators, and an occasional armadillo. Recently there have been several sightings of the South Florida manatee.

Years ago, the hotel and golf course owners put Myrtle Beach on the map with the introduction of the "golf package." Until then, golf resorts ran themselves like exclusive country clubs. This practice is still prevalent in most of the country, but down here the owners have gotten together to make golf not only available but affordable. As a consequence, when you check in at a hotel you are automatically guaranteed golf course privileges on almost any of the courses in the area. Golf packages, high-quality courses, and the weather have combined to make Myrtle Beach the most popular golf destination in the world.

BUT! There's always a but. You can't just check into any hotel and get the full golf package. So you'll have to do a little spadework to find out exactly what courses are available on your particular package.

Choosing a hotel and golf package is easier with the help of the Myrtle Beach Chamber of Commerce. Call them at (800) 356–3016 or write Myrtle Beach Area Chamber of Commerce, P.O. Box 2115, Myrtle Beach 29578. They'll send you, free of charge, an elaborate 313-page magazine of hotel, golf course, restaurant, and nightclub information. Called the *Stay & Play Guide,* it can answer all of your questions about where to stay and exactly which golf courses come with each package.

In the center of Myrtle Beach is **The Pavilion,** which is the spot where Beach Music and The Shag Dance were born. This is also the spot where all the aforementioned graduates congregate every June. At night the place looks like Vegas, with its cartoon-colored neon lights and the carnival noises from the Ferris wheel, the roller coaster, and other rides across the street. Kids love it here and won't want to leave. If the action gets rowdy, the police are friendly and used to handling the problems.

Barefoot Landing, 4898 Highway 17 South, North Myrtle Beach 29582, is a 120-shop-and-restaurant complex built on and out over the Intracoastal Waterway. The shops and restaurants here are built of weathered cypress-like wood and decorated with bright green awnings. Children can ride a European-style carousel. The entire area is pleasant to stroll around and watch the ducks and the big fish in the river. Children love this area and can be turned loose to explore. Call (800) 272–2320.

A great spot to have a cold one at night on Barefoot Landing on Route 17, 11 miles south of the North Carolina border, is the famous *House of Blues* at 4640 Highway 17 South, North Myrtle Beach 29582. This is the number one spot in S.C. for blues. One of the big stars here, from Pomaria, S.C., is Nathanial Nappy Brown who is a one of a kind wonder. Nappy wrote many of the hot blues numbers that are still with us. He has been, and still is, friends with Chuck Berry, B. B. King, Ray Charles, The Beatles, etc., and doesn't mind sitting down with you and telling you everything he knows about them and their music. The restaurant is open from 8:00 A.M. until 1:00 A.M. daily. Ticket prices are $30 for a full meal and show. Call (843) 272–3000.

Cruises on the Waterway aboard the *Barefoot Princess* originate from here. They are so popular during the height of the season and on holidays that the boat operates on a first-come, first-served basis at these times. At other times you can call for a reservation at (843) 272–7743.

The *Dixie Stampede* is a 1,000-seat theater owned by Dolly Parton. The added attraction here is you can eat a full meal while you watch the show. These shows are one of the biggest successes in the area and keep getting bigger and bigger. If you come down be sure to catch at least one. Frankly, they are all a little bit the same. But that's all right, because the stars are all professionals and go all out to put on a good show. The theaters are high-tech and state-of-the-art. Between acts performers sit on the edge of the stage and talk to the crowd. The price for adults is $32.99; $16.99 for children ages three to eleven; free for children under three on a parent's lap. For reservations and information call (800) 433–4401.

Music

*N*ot only is South Carolina the birthplace of Beach Music and such groups as The Platters, The Coasters, and The Drifters, it's right up there at the top in blues and bluegrass. For blues, try the House of Blues at Barefoot Landing. As for bluegrass, it's best on an AM station, preferably on one of the hundred back roads that don't make the cut on most maps. If you hear the same music in a New York or Chicago traffic jam it's just not the same. It's not even close. But when you get on some old Carolina tar and gravel road, with the mules and the cotton and the "R.U. Ready For Eternity" painted on automobile tires and nailed to the fence posts, and the dogs are all standing around in threes and fours, I guarantee it's going to make a big, big difference. Don't laugh until you try it.

Myrtle Beach is the Putt-Putt Capital of the known world. It also has a 20,000-square-foot wave pool, and for a few bucks you can take a helicopter ride around the area or parasail up and down the beach.

Ristorante Villa Romana at 707 South King's Highway, Myrtle Beach 29577, is open for dinner seven days a week. A delightful place to dine, Villa Romana has strolling violinists and a gypsy accordionist. Often Mama Lucia, overcome by Puccini or Verdi, will dance and sway among the tables. The specialties here are traditional Italian recipes; they serve probably the best veal in the area. The soups, pasta, and bread are all made fresh daily. Prices range from $15 to $25. Call (843) 448–4990.

Myrtle Beach State Park, located at 4401 South King's Highway, is one of forty-eight state parks in South Carolina. They can be written to at the above address or reached by phone at (843) 238–5325. Currently they have available here in the Myrtle Beach area the following accommodations: five cabins (each sleeps six) at $73.37 during the summer, per cabin per night, and $52.56 off-season, per cabin per night. Two apartments (each sleeps four) at $48.18 per night during the summer, and $42.71 per night off-season, and 350 campsites at $22 a night from April 1 through October 31 and $18.60 a night from November 1 through March 31. Prices subject to change. Call for current rates.

If you would like further information on any or all of the forty-eight parks in the state, please write South Carolina State Parks, c/o Kay White, 1205 Pendelton Street, Columbia 29201. The parks are famous for their fireplace-equipped cabins, their beautiful settings, nature hikes, golf courses, and fishing expeditions. Needless to say, this is a nonprofit operation, and it offers a wonderful way to visit and vacation at very reasonable prices.

Downtown in Myrtle Beach in the heart of the heart of it all is *Ripley's Believe It or Not* (901 North Ocean Boulevard, Myrtle Beach 29577). If you haven't been here yet don't miss it this time. It's endless, incomprehensible, and amazing.

Some of the hotter tickets at Ripley's are "Three-Ball Charlie"— the man who could put three balls in his mouth (tennis ball, golf ball, billiard ball) and whistle at the same time—a genuine Jivaro shrunken head from Ecuador, a two-headed calf, and a mock graveyard with an R.I.P. stone engraved:

> HERE LIES AN ATHEIST,
> ALL DRESSED UP AND
> NO PLACE TO GO.

And who could forget "Kamala, the wolf girl, raised in the jungles of India by wolves."

Kids love this place; if you let them, they'll stay here all day. Prices are $9.75 for adults, $6.50 for kids ages six to twelve, free for kids under six. If you save your ticket, you get a dollar off on a pizza next door at *The Pizza Place.* Ripley's is open 10:00 A.M. to 10:00 P.M. daily year-round. Call (843) 448–2331.

Across the street, at 916 North Boulevard, Myrtle Beach 29577, is the *Gay Dolphin Incorporated,* which simply defies description. You literally have to go here to believe it. Every conceivable shell design, every T-shirt, every possible item of tacky and not-so-tacky mantelpiece memorabilia, whatnot, wall hanging, and bumper sticker in the Western world is here. And the place is cavernous. My favorite bumper sticker is I DON'T CALL 911. They also carry some pretty funny postcards. One is a pitch-black card with the caption "Myrtle Beach at Midnight." Be sure to stop here. It's a standing bet, even money, that you won't leave until you buy something. Summer hours Easter through Labor Day are 9:30 A.M. to 11:30 P.M. Monday through Thursday, 9:30 A.M. until midnight Friday and Saturday, and 9:30 A.M. to 11:30 P.M. Sunday. After Labor Day, open daily 9:00 A.M. to 5:30 P.M. Call (843) 448–6550.

There are a couple of house rules on Myrtle Beach. Dogs must be on a leash at all times. No animals are allowed on the beach or Ocean Boulevard between Twenty-first Avenue North to Thirteenth Avenue South during any time of the year. No dogs are allowed on the beach between 9:00 A.M. and 5:00 P.M. from May 15 through September 15.

Riding horses on the beach is allowed from November 12 through February 27. A few miles south, at Surfside, you can ride from November 2 through March 31.

Up on the end of Route 17 is the Little River area, which is famous for Calabash-style seafood and a wealth of brand-new and exciting golf courses. Right in the middle of Little River is *Tidewater Golf Club and Plantation,* named in 1990 the best new public course in the country by *Golf Magazine* and *Golf Digest.* Once again, this is a public course open to almost anyone with a set of sticks. All you have to do is call (843) 249–3829 for a tee time and bring plenty of balls for the water holes.

The great secret of Tidewater's unique success lies with Ken Tomlinson, the owner and course designer. He has laid out multiple landing areas for each tee, a design feature which allows players of every level to play the same iron from fairway to green on each hole. Another of Ken's wise decisions here at Tidewater is that he has given the course the best land possible—the high, wooded peninsula that lies between the Atlantic Ocean and the Intracoastal Waterway. And still another feature of the course is that Ken doesn't believe in the dreary ninety-degree use of carts on the fairways. On most days you can drive them right down the middle and save yourself a lot of club carrying and unnecessary walking. Ken says, "Hell, it's only grass." This is a superb course and it stays in beautiful shape. For further information write Tidewater Golf Club and Plantation, 4901 Little River Neck Road, North Myrtle Beach 29582. Call (800) 446–5363, or fax (843) 249–5281.

On Route 501 past Conway and Aynor you'll come to the **Galivants Ferry Convenience Store.** Right here is the center for the 114-year-old stump-meeting convention that occurs here every June. The organizer is one John Monroe Holliday, who also oversees the largest tobacco farm in operation in South Carolina as well as a number of diverse business interests throughout Horry County.

In 1979 the Hollidays were honored for their contribution to the economic progress of the area and for their public service to South Carolina by the Department of Highways and Public Transportation. The section of U.S. 501 between Galivants Ferry and Conway was renamed The Holliday Highway.

John Holliday, his brother Joseph, and their families have been personally responsible for continuing a tradition their grandfather began in 1880—"The Galivants Ferry Democratic Stump Speaking." John Holliday says, "I remember sitting on a wagon in a thicket, drinking cherry cola while fifty to seventy-five people stood on a stump or some boards to speak. The Stump started when there was only a Democratic party in the state. We didn't even know how to spell Republican."

John and his brother Joseph have continued another tradition started by their grandfather. Each of them has been the postmaster of Galivants Ferry.

A stop here at the convenience store right on the highway and a chance to meet John Holliday or one of his family, who will tell you all about the place and certainly invite you to the June meeting, is definitely a once-in-a-lifetime experience.

Okay, excluding my every meal at home, the best meal I've had all year was at **Daruma Japanese House,** King's Highway, North Myrtle Beach 29572 (843–497–6038). I still don't know what it was but it started off with hot sake and green soy beans that you open with your fingers, much like boiled peanuts. Then a gondola with a cascade of sushi and tempura, with at least nine different exotic tastes, had my senses reeling. I actually found myself humming while I ate. The place is about as Japanese as it gets. The owner is moving to Route 17 in Murrells Inlet—Mickey Spillane country—but the loyal followers all swear they will gladly drive the 20-odd miles down the road. As for me, if I have to, I'll drive the 140 miles or more.

The owner, an avid golfer, will talk your head off about golf. He's much more interesting if you ask about the knives he uses to cut up the sushi. They range in price from $40 to $1,000. And listen to this! The whetstones used to keep them sharp range in price from $300 to $3,000.

The *Original Benjamin's Calabash Seafood and Nautical Museum,* located at 9593 North Kings Highway, Myrtle Beach, 29572, is a one-of-a-kind masterpiece. It offers a 170-item buffet with crab legs; Oriental, Italian, and country food, seafood, soup, salad, and dessert bars; and can seat and serve over 500 guests at a time. As you first enter the restaurant you will see the world's largest model of the *Queen Elizabeth,* the actual one that was shown to the Queen before the ship was built in her honor. Next you will see the dry sea aquarium, which houses the largest collection of mounted fish in the Southeast. As advertised, all the fish were alive at one time. You will also see the largest replica of the *Mayflower.* The rest of the lobby and the many rooms that make up

A Sample of North Carolina

*L*et's face it, Myrtle Beach is getting crowded. So is North Myrtle Beach. If you want to play golf, stay at a great place, be on the ocean, and get away from the traffic and bustle, all you have to do is drive 8–10 miles north of Tidewater Golf Club and Plantation in Little River (see pages 75–76). You can cross the North Carolina line without a passport. And the natives are friendly.

A great spot to stop and look around would be **Ocean Isle Beach** and the **Ocean Isle Inn,** at 37 West First Street, Ocean Isle Beach 28469. Call (800) 352–5988 or (910) 579–0750. From here you are within ten minutes of thirty-six championship golf courses in North and South Carolina, and some of the finest food and fishing in the world. Unlike most East Coast beaches, which run north–south, Ocean Island is east–west oriented, which lets you see some of the most incredible sunrises and sunsets imaginable. This is the perfect place for family vacations, reunions, club outings, or romantic getaways.

The premiere course here is the Ocean Isle Beach Golf Course, where I have played many times. I am here to tell you, it's wonderful.

Benjamin's Original Calabash are filled with compasses, telescopes, underwater cameras, buoys, anchors, aquariums and much, much more. There is also a full-sized shark hanging outside the front door. In other words, Benjamin's Calabash Restaurant has to be seen to be believed. And the food and service is probably the best on the beach.

Caution, this is the original Benjamin's Calabash. There are other Calabashes along the beach, and a few are even using the names Ben and Benjamin's. But in the words of the circus, "Be not deceived by envious competitors." All you have to do is try the Original Benjamin's and you will stray no farther.

For reservations call (800) 288–8687. Open daily May through September from 2:30 P.M. to whenever dinner is over. Open at 3:30 P.M. from October through April. For further information, visit Benjamin's at www.originalbenjamins.com.

Another fine Inn on the beach is *The Islander Inn* at 57 West First Street, Ocean Isle Beach 28469, offering the very finest lodging, accommodations, and expert assistance for the golf enthusiast. Highly recommended are the Pearl Course and Angels Trace. I've played both, and they are outstanding. The inn features indoor and outdoor pools as well as a first-class spa. In case you think you're too far north of South Carolina, keep in mind you're only 10 miles from Little River. Call them at (888) 325–4753 or (910) 575–7000; fax: (910) 575–7075; www. Islanderinn.com.

Stop at *Victoria's Restaurant and Sports Bar* at 125 Causeway Drive, Ocean Isle Beach 28469, for homemade crab cakes and snow crab legs. They also serve a delicious 12-ounce rib eye and 10-ounce filet mignon. This casual neighborhood watering hole comes complete with dart boards, pool table, and eleven—count them—TV screens. A great spot to relax, eat, and watch your favorite game. Live entertainment on weekends. Open daily; call (910) 575–4746 for hours.

The *Museum of Coastal Carolina,* the area's premier museum of natural history, is located at 21 East Second Street, Ocean Isle Beach 28469. It is an ideal place to bring the family, especially the kids. Every day at 2:00 P.M. there is a nature program and/or storytime. Topics include snakes, alligators, fossils, shells, birds of prey, fish and fishing, and Native American lore. For small children, there is a hands-on-activity area, complete with bones, shells, skulls, hides, and magnification devices. In addition there is a Loggerhead Turtle Watch every evening at 7:00 P.M. Summer hours begin Memorial Day and end Labor Day. Open the rest of the year Friday and Saturday 9:00 A.M.–5:00 P.M. and Sunday 1:00–5:00 P.M. Call (910) 579–1016.

Goose Creek Bed and Breakfast at 1901 Egret Street Ocean Isle 28469, is perfect, located right in the heart of Ocean Isle. There is a pier that gives you access to fishing and, if you bring a canoe or a kayak, you can fish the waters of the Intracoastal Waterway. What better way to spend a vacation? Rates range from $80 to $100 per night in-season and $70 to $90 per night off-season. Special golf packages are available. Call (800) 275–6540 or write to Jim and Peggy Grich at the above address or www.goosecreekbb.com.

Ten miles north of Ocean Isle, go to Southport and pick up the ferry to one of the most amazing and most beautiful islands in the Atlantic—***Bald Head Island,*** N.C. Departing from Indigo Plantation on West Ninth Street in Southport (telephone 910–457–5003) you will go out to the island, go on the tour, have lunch and return. The fee is $15.00 per adult, $8.00 per child under twelve. While out on Bald Head you can look over the very fine golf course and the accommodations, see the famous Old Baldy Lighthouse, and decide when you want to come back and spend a few days. Most of this remarkable island has been given over to the state wildlife commission and is now a bird and turtle sanctuary. It also has one of the finest stands of live oaks and maritime forests on the coast. Pelicans and giant herons are everywhere and at night there is a good chance you will see a loggerhead. Another bonus is that there are no cars except maintenance vehicles. If you are going to do one thing and one thing only in N.C., here's what you do. Go to Bald Head, play eighteen holes on the truly great course lined with live oaks, herons, egrets, pelicans, and almost any kind of wildlife you can imagine. Then have a cool one at the bar overlooking the rocks and surf while you watch the sun slowly set and luxuriously reflect on what a great day it has been and how you might just very well stay.

Dillon

Nearby at Highway 301 and I–95, Hamer 29547 (843–774–2411), is **South of the Border** (or SOB, as it's known to insiders), an amalgam of South Carolina and Old Mexico—a yellow and pink Tijuana backed in black velvet. Pedro, a 97-foot statue, straddles the entrance and is billed as "the largest free-standing sign east of the Mississippi."

You can drive in between his legs. Inside they have the biggest, brightest, tackiest assortment of what is affectionately called memorabilia, which runs the gamut from eight types of back-scratchers to at least thirty, and still counting, types of coffee mugs. They also have flags of every description, clever bumper stickers, tapes, CDs, and wood cuts of "God Bless Our Mortgaged Home."

Under Pedro's magnificent sombrero, billed as the Eiffel Tower of the South, dozens of weddings take place every summer. For $160 you can get married and spend a night in an "heir-conditioned" honeymoon suite complete with champagne, a water bed, and a free breakfast, which isn't a bad way to start a married life. South Carolinians claim they wouldn't be caught dead here, but the place is packed and if you want a room you'll have to call in advance for a reservation. Call (843) 774–2411.

PLACES TO STAY IN THE GRAND STRAND

GEORGETOWN
Mansfield Plantation
1776 Mansfield Road
Georgetown 29440
(843) 546–6961

Shaw House
613 Cypress Court
Georgetown 29440
(843) 546–9663

MCCLELLANVILLE
Laurel Hill Plantation
McClellanville 29458
(843) 887–3708

MONCK'S CORNER
Rice Hope Plantation Inn
Mepkin Abbey Road
Monck's Corner 29461
(843) 761–4832

MYRTLE BEACH
Brustman House
400 25th Avenue South
Myrtle Beach 29577
(843) 448–7699

PAWLEYS ISLAND
Litchfield Plantation
P.O. Box 320
Pawleys Island 29585
(843) 237–5300

PLACES TO EAT IN THE GRAND STRAND

MURRELLS INLET
Nance's Creek Front Restaurant
Highway 17 Business
Murrells Inlet 29576
(843) 651–2696

Oliver's Lodge
4204 Highway 17 Business
Murrells Inlet 29576
(843) 651–2963

Inlet House Cafe
Highway 17 Murrells Inlet
Murrells Inlet 29576
(843) 651–0622

MYRTLE BEACH
Nibil's at Surfside Pier
11 South Ocean Boulevard
Surfside 29575
(843) 238–5080

PAWLEYS ISLAND
Tyler's Cove Restaurant
10880 Ocean Highway
Pawleys Island 29585
(843) 237–4848

The Fall Line

Tobacco and Cotton Lands

outh Carolina is roughly a triangle covering 30,000 square miles, 500 of which are inland lakes. From the northwest corner, near the Chatooga River, a rough and jagged line runs east for 330 miles to Little River Inlet, marking the boundary between South and North Carolina. To the west, the Savannah River extends southeast from that same northwest corner for 240 miles to Tybee Sound, which separates the state from Georgia and lies adjacent to Savannah. And on the east coast, the Atlantic shoreline stretches roughly 200 miles between Little River and Tybee Sound. The state is drained by three main river systems: the Pee Dee in the northeast, the Santee in the central area, and the Savannah in the southeast. The swift flow of the rivers in the Upcountry has led most of the state's manufacturing plants to select sites in that section. Below the fall line—which runs across the state and separates the Up from the Low—these red, mud-laden rivers become wide and clear, depositing their silt on the bottom. Stained black with tannic acid from cypress and other roots, the rivers run slowly on under the live oaks and tupelos through the flat, rich soils to the Atlantic Ocean.

The area in the northeast around the muddy Pee Dee River is called the Pee Dee section, and right in the middle is the city of *Florence.* The city is in the heart of the tobacco region of the state, and every fall the annual Tobacco Jubilee is an important event of the Pee Dee Fair. A visit to the city, which is 65 miles from the coast, is interesting in that it shows how an old downtown section of a small town can still compete with a brand-new sprawling mall a few miles away.

Barringer Hardware, on Evans Street, is about 150 feet deep, and every square inch is covered with merchandise. Fan belts and parts of plows hang from rafters, and if you look hard enough you can find two different sizes of old-fashioned scrub boards for washing clothes. Jack Barringer, the owner, also sells fireplace equipment, copper tubing, wet mops, paints, iron skillets, about two dozen different kinds of brushes,

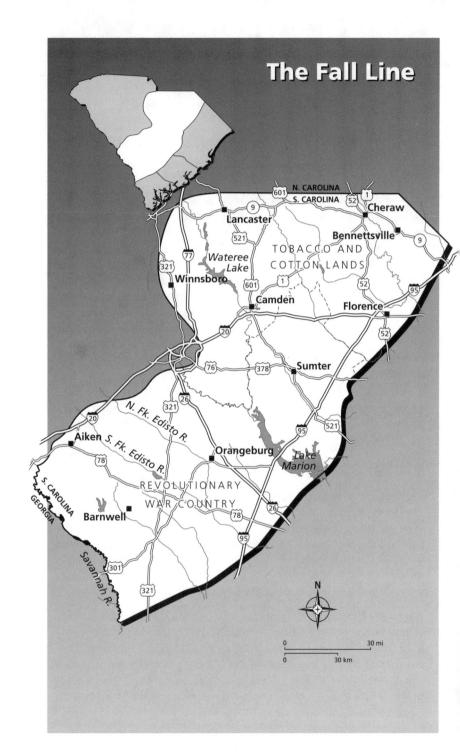

The Fall Line

N. CAROLINA
S. CAROLINA

Cheraw

Lancaster

Bennettsville

TOBACCO AND
COTTON LANDS

Wateree
Lake

Winnsboro

Camden

Florence

Sumter

N. Fk. Edisto R.

Aiken

S. Fk. Edisto R.

Orangeburg

Lake
Marion

REVOLUTIONARY
WAR COUNTRY

S. CAROLINA
GEORGIA

Barnwell

Savannah R.

N

0   30 mi
0   30 km

THE FALL LINE

and a galvanized double tub suitable for bathing a not-very-large person. Up in his office he has a poster from years ago advertising buggy and wagon parts. Jack is easygoing and easy to talk to. If you have any questions about Florence, he'll be glad to answer them.

Florence has been nicknamed "Tooth City," "Tooth Capital," and "Denture Capital of the World" due to the reputation of the **Sexton Dental Clinic,** at 377 West Palmetto Street, Florence 29501. It advertises "affordable general dentistry," so people come from as far away as Hawaii and Alaska because of the low prices and the fact that work is done by the assembly-line method and almost anything, even full dentures top and bottom, can be done right here in one day. They're open Monday through Friday from 6:00 A.M. to 5:00 P.M. For emergencies, they are open twenty-four hours a day, seven days a week. They accept major credit cards. Call (843) 662–2543. While you're waiting for your dentures, you can visit the **Sexton Vision Center** for an eye examination right across the street from the dental clinic. They have rock-bottom prices on glasses and sunglasses.

The Columns, right outside Florence, was built in the 1850s and is a fine example of the Greek Revival architecture popular among plantation homes of the antebellum South. The Columns remains a working plantation operated by offspring of its original owners and is listed on the National Register of Historic Places. Civil War reenactments are held biannually on its grounds. Tours are available by appointment. Call (843) 664–6730, or fax (843) 667–1351.

At lunchtime, head to **Red Bone Alley** at 1903 West Palmetto Street, Florence 29501. This is an amazing combination restaurant, bar, sports bar, and game room. The ceiling is at least 30 feet high, and you are surrounded by sides of houses depicting the various styles of architecture that characterize Charleston, Williamsburg, San Francisco, and so on. They serve a very good lunch here for $9.00; dinners are around $15.00.

The game room features a CD jukebox with more than 1,000 selections. Three pool tables and an air hockey setup are also here. One of the pool tables is L-shaped with eight pockets. Weird. You must be over twenty-one to use the game room, or you must be accompanied by an adult or parent. Call (843) 673–0035.

After lunch, be sure to stop by the **Florence Museum of Art, Science, and History,** if for no other reason than to see the extraordinary work of William Henry Johnson, who painted here in 1940. His childlike but incredibly moving painting *Evening* was painted on rough burlap and may be in Columbia being restored when you get here, but his *Christmas Party* and *Rooftops of Denmark* are here year-round. Picasso once said it took him twenty years to learn to paint like Rembrandt but all his life to learn to paint like a child. Picasso would have loved Johnson's work. The museum is located at 558 Spruce Street, Florence 29501. Open Tuesday through Saturday 10:00 A.M. to 5:00 P.M., Sunday 2:00 to 5:00 P.M. And it's all free. Call (843) 662–3351.

Northeast of Florence, 15 miles away, is Darlington, founded in 1785 and the home of the Darlington 500 motor race, which is held every Labor Day. In the center of the town is a giant mural 100 feet long and 20 feet high painted by Blue Sky, a Columbia artist whose work can be found all over the state. The mural is a rendering of how the old city looked at the turn of the century when a huge oak was the centerpiece of the old town square.

Lee State Park is only 7 miles away on the banks of the Lynches River at 487 Loop Road, Bishopville 29010. The park is open all year and is especially suited for horseback riding. Although they don't provide horses, they do have a stable, a very fine bridle path, and a show ring. Walking-around admission is free; campsites are $12 per night. Call (803) 428–5307. It was here in 1880 that the last duel in the state was fought. The contestants were Colonel William S. Shannon of Camden and Colonel E. B. C. Cash of Cheraw. They met at Dubose's Bridge, which was in neutral territory. Colonel Shannon was mortally wounded, and his death resulted in a state law against dueling. Even today, South Carolina officials must swear they have not engaged in a duel since January 1, 1881, and that they will not engage in dueling during their term of office.

An even more flamboyant episode in Pee Dee country history was the "Darlington War" of 1894. This was an outbreak caused by Governor B. R. "Pitchfork Ben" Tillman's liquor regulations, particularly his order permitting private

---

The Importance of Fat

I once asked an owner of a West Coast salmon packing company why red salmon tasted so good and pink so sorry. His answer was the simple and straightforward, "We remove the fat from the pink." Well, down here we don't remove the fat. My Dad once pronounced that "Grease was the secret of the South. When you take it out, all you're doing is ruining it."

I said, "Ruining what?"

And he said, "Everything."

homes to be searched without warrant for concealed liquor. In the first skirmish two citizens and one constable were killed, and a number of others were injured. A day later Darlingtonians fired on a train bringing in more constables and began scouring the countryside for other lawmen. Tillman countered by bringing in the militia, but many companies refused to obey and were dishonorably discharged. Among these was the Charleston company, whose members declined to surrender their arms and went on to defend their action in Federal court against "one B. R. Tillman, styling himself Governor of South Carolina." Tillman finally collected more docile troops, but by this time the Darlington Guards, a local vigilante group, had restored the peace.

The *Darlington County Historical Commission* is housed in the old city jail at 204 Hewitt Street, Darlington 29532. Inside are wonderful photographs from more than 100 years ago that portray the history of the town, the growth and decline of the cotton empire, the introduction of the automobile, and other notable events and facts. Also on exhibit are Stephen Foster's original lyrics for "Way Down upon the Swanee River." Originally the river was the Pee Dee, which runs nearby, and you can see where he scratched it out on the manuscript and changed it to Swanee. No one seems to know why. Hours are 9:00 A.M. to 5:00 P.M. No admission charge. Phone (843) 398–4710.

The *Darlington Speedway* on Route 52 is so big and commanding there is no way to miss it. Inside the main gate is an interesting museum that features fifteen old racing cars. Each car is equipped with an audio module that tells the history of the car, where and when it ran, and who drove it. Also available is every conceivable piece of memorabilia you can think of, from jackets and caps to postcards and testimonials from famous drivers. Admission is $3.00 for adults; children under twelve are admitted free. Open Monday through Saturday from 9:00 A.M. to 6:00 P.M. Call (843) 395–8449.

If you'd like to see a race, the two big racing weekends are late March and Labor Day, when the big Darlington 500 is run. For those who would just like to see the track, walk down to the white security building at the end of the fence that runs along the front. The guard there will give you permission to climb up the short walk, where you can see the great expanse of curving concrete that is the track. You can also see the stands and the giant billboards. It's a sight you won't soon forget.

Outside Bishopville on I–20 heading east you'll come to a series of cotton and soybean fields that are as flat as a parking lot. Right in the middle at Charlene Lane, Bishopville, 29010 is a big 6-foot-high red

Roadside Signs

Near Winnsboro a grocery store sign reads simply DE STO.

neon sign spelling out simply EAT. It's one of those signs you wonder about. Well, pull off and stop by here. The food is down-home southern and very good. The new name is **Charlene's Taste of Country,** and they specialize in fried chicken, country-fried steak, great fresh vegetables, and lush desserts. Prices are low, from $6.00 to $9.00. Call (803) 428–2900.

One of the older and prouder Upcountry towns is Winnsboro, the seat of Fairfield County. It was settled in 1755 and named for Colonel Richard Winn, Revolutionary officer and early town father. Pennsylvanians and North Carolinians settled here, but along with them came many from the Low Country who were seeking a more healthful climate and broader cotton lands.

Thirty years ago at the corner of Congress and Washington stood a Confederate monument of a lone soldier facing north. After a few of the local "tosspots" banged their Fords and Chevys into it and tried to climb it, it was moved to the park two blocks away. Needless to say, the city fathers saw to it that the soldier still faces north.

The centerpiece of this old town, along with its Confederate soldier, is the town clock and belfry at the corner of Washington and Main. The bell was used as an alarm for fires and curfew and to let the villagers know that fresh meat was available. Tradition has it that there were beaten paths from every direction made by dogs who knew that the sound of the bell meant fresh meat for them as well as their masters.

The bell for the clock was made in France, and the story goes that for a long time it had a clear and silvery tone. In 1895, during a fire, it was rung so vigorously it cracked and had to be sent to Philadelphia for repairs. When it was finally returned, the old-timers reported it had lost its silvery tone, and it was doubtful whether or not it was the original bell. In spite of the cracked bell and the shoddy northern repairs, the old clock is the longest continuously running town clock in the United States.

On weekends you might try **The News and Herald Tavern Restaurant,** at 114 East Washington Street, Winnsboro 29180 (803–635–1331). It's so close to the railroad tracks the glasses shake when the train comes through. The food is very good, with prices ranging from $6.00 to $15.00. Baking and dessert preparation are all done on the premises. All vegetables are fresh. Currently, the Tavern is open Monday through Saturday, closed on Sunday.

Heading east on Route 34 you'll be through the community of Rockton before you realize it. As a matter of fact, the railroad crossing is the community. On the immediate right you'll see an outdoor museum with no one in attendance. It's the *Fairfield County, South Carolina Railroad Museum.* If you're a railroad buff you can stop and look over the old steam engines and cabooses; they even have a 1930 day coach. Every year a new train or caboose or old engine is added to the collection. And every fall an old-fashioned steam engine cranks up and pulls a few day coach cars up into the mountains for a look at the changing of the leaves. This is a fascinating trip, but since there is no published departure schedule you will have to phone the Winnsboro Chamber of Commerce at (803) 635–4242 for details.

On Route 34 coming into the town of Ridgeway you might stop at the *Letterbox Café,* formerly *"Maw's Kitchen."* Maw is still there. She has only three tables and six booths, but she runs a tight ship. Breakfasts of sausage, grits, and eggs are especially good. So are her BLTs and bologna sandwiches. Open from 6:00 A.M. to 9:00 P.M. Monday through Saturday, closed Sunday. Call (803) 337–3287.

The *Thomas Store,* built in 1885, on Main Street in the center of town, is owned by one Laura Thomas, who is also the mayor. Even though most of her family have graduated from Sewanee and Harvard and gone on to other professions, they all come back once in a while and help out behind the counter.

The store is a beauty, with enormous windows, a skylight, and 16-foot ceilings made of ornamental tin. Thomas is proud of her glass showcase, which contains two or three dozen kinds of hats, and her 100-

Roadside Facts

In small towns there is no law against dogs running loose, and every night you'll see three, four, and five gathering at night under the street lights and planning their evening. When we lived in Winnsboro, right up the road from Columbia, nine of them wound up living on our porch. I, like a fool, not only bought them food but paid their vet bills and bought them couches and overstuffed chairs from the Salvation Army. One was named Zeke, a direct descendant of one of the somersaulting terriers from the Hunt Brothers Circus, which used to have their winter quarters up the road in Gaffney. At night all nine would line up in full chorus when the trains went through at 2:00 and 4:00 in the morning, and it was the most god-awful beautiful sound I will ever hear.

year-old hoop cheese cutter. You can buy a slice of cheese here from a giant hoop that fits in the cutter. She'll cut it for you. Also for sale are shoes, overalls, and appliances ranging from toasters and electric can openers to deep freezers and refrigerators. On the second floor she has a heavy cardboard display of the old Victor record dog. Everyone wants to buy it, but she's not selling. Open 9:00 A.M. to 5:00 P.M. Closed Sunday.

Be sure to see the **Old Town Hall** and take the three-block walking tour of the town and its **antebellum and Victorian houses.** Directly across the street from the Thomas Store is a beautiful Victorian home constructed by Robert Charleton Thomas in 1906. Note the mounting block in the corner of the front yard. This large block of granite allowed young ladies to step delicately into their awaiting carriages.

The **Augustus Tally Moore House** was built in 1899. Mr. Moore's young son was so distressed at seeing a local crippled man that he swore to repair the foot one day. A. T. Moore grew up to become a fine doctor, and he perfected and patented the first artificial hip socket. The first surgery he performed was to repair the foot of the crippled man he had seen as a child.

The **Charles Wray House** on Peach Street at the corner of Highway 34 is an enormous and imposing home. Residents say if you to look carefully at the attic windows you may see Charles Wray, who built this home in 1910, staring down the railroad tracks in search of his wife and child, who were killed with him in a tragic train accident.

Revolutionary War Country

*H*ighway 34 east takes you back into Camden. Established in 1732, it is the oldest inland town in the state. For nearly a century Camden was noted for its duels and was the mecca for gentlemen seeking instructions in the code of honor, but this era came to a close in 1880 when dueling was outlawed after the Cash-Shannon duel in Darlington. In 1791, at the corner of Bull and Broad Streets, Washington addressed the local citizens, but what he said has been lost in the mists of history.

The approach to the town is over the Wateree River Bridge and then through a half mile of luxurious magnolia trees that seem to stay in bloom all spring and summer. Camden is the home of **The Carolina Cup Steeplechase** in April and **The Colonial Cup Steeplechase** in November. If you're here during these times you can watch the natives drinking champagne as they motor out to the track in their antique cars. Arriving here, they will often spread out an enormous Oriental rug and, after securing the corners with huge vases of cut flowers, arrange a fine silver and crystal picnic in the middle of the infield. Once in a while a group will outdo all the others by showing up in elaborate evening clothes accompanied by a string quartet and, I'm not kidding, a chandelier. If you're interested in attending this event, call the Kershaw County Chamber of Commerce at (803) 432–2525. It's located at 724 South Broad Street, Camden 29020.

The *Historic Camden Revolutionary War Site,* located at 200 Broad Street, is a ninety-eight-acre museum open seven days a week, except major holidays. This is the site of the original town of Camden, which was fortified by the British in 1780. Portions of the palisade walls have been rebuilt where they originally stood. The old mansion, built on the war site by Joseph Kershaw, one of the town fathers, was used as British Headquarters during the occupation. It has been reconstructed and can be seen on any of the walking tours of the area.

For a walking tour of Camden call (803) 432–2525. A quicker, more romantic tour in a horse-drawn carriage can be very colorful. For information, write to the Camden Carriage Company, P.O. Box 1082, Camden 29020 or call them at (803) 425–5737. Most of the sixty-odd houses seen on either the walking tour or the carriage tour are private homes and may only be viewed from the street. A few, however, are available for interior tours. Check with the Kershaw County Chamber of Commerce for this information. Call (803) 432–2525 or write them at 724 South Broad Street, Camden 29020.

For an excellent bed-and-breakfast in downtown Camden, *The Greenleaf,* located at 1308 North Broad, Camden 29020, is at the head of the list. Call (803) 425–1806. Dinner prices at the grill range from $15 to $30 with an elaborate dessert followed by coffee, cognac, and hand-rolled cigars out on the veranda.

In September 1989 Hurricane Hugo hit not only the Carolina coast but, to everyone's surprise, came barreling inland with winds of over 110 miles an hour through Sumter, Camden, and all the way up to Charlotte. Camden's big trailer park a few miles to the south of the center of town was devastated; most of the units were completely destroyed. The damage has been repaired, but every September and October people around here begin checking the weather reports and keeping a wary eye on the sky. A calypso song from the Low Country by way of Barbados tells us the months to watch.

The Patriot and South Carolina

*I*t wasn't until I saw Mel Gibson in The Patriot—an excellent movie that should be required viewing for every South Carolina native—and reread my history that I discovered South Carolina had 245 skirmishes and battles during the Revolutionary War. In fact, most of the war was fought right here. Some of this truly beautiful movie was shot down in the swamps and plantations of the Low Country around Charleston and Beaufort, but most of it was filmed upstate, where much of the war took place. If you're interested in history, the Camden-Winnsboro area 30 miles north of Columbia would be the ideal place to trace most of the action and events. As a matter of fact, at the Historic Camden Revolutionary War Site, located 1.4 miles from I–20 on the outskirts of Camden, they offer guided interactive tours, complete with a videotape made by SC ETV about the Battle of Camden. Only a mile away you can visit the Baron De Kalb Memorial, designed by Robert Mills, who also designed the Washington Monument. Dekalb was the German-born French citizen who became a general in the Continental Army and was mortally wounded during the Battle of Camden. He is buried at a downtown church. The two major battles fought here—the Battle of Camden and the Battle of Hobkirk Hill— resulted in British General Cornwallis's retreat north and his eventual surrender to Washington at Yorktown, Virginia in October 1781.

Before you visit the old Palmetto State, I'd strongly suggest you see this popular and very fine movie.

JUNE TOO SOON
JULY STAND BY
AUGUST ALMOST
SEPTEMBER REMEMBER
OCTOBER NOT OVER

You might need some sustenance after a walking or carriage tour, so head to the **Old South Restaurant** at 402 De Kalb Street, Camden 29020. Although Camden is 100 miles from the coast, the shrimp here is firm and fresh and always available. The Plantation Chicken, a chicken breast stuffed with oyster and corn-bread dressing and drizzled with a light creamy sauce, is especially good and comes with a little item called Johnny's Stuffed Potato. For dessert, there's chocolate cake and coffee. The total price, including tip, will be about $24, and you'll have a very fine meal. Dinner is served Tuesday to Thursday from 5:30 to 9:00 P.M. and on Friday and Saturday from 5:30 to 10:00 P.M. Lunch is served Tuesday through Saturday from 11:30 A.M. to 2:30 P.M.

One of the best reasons for visiting Camden is to get your bearings and be able to find the town of *Boykin* about 20 miles away. Take Route 521 south and turn right at Route 261; drive 4 miles or so. And there you are—that is, if you haven't missed it. It's on the left side of the road, and you have to watch for it.

The millpond and other properties here are owned by the heirs of Lemuel Whitaker Boykin II, six generations from the original 1775 settler, William Boykin II. The entire community, which consists of the General Store, the Broom Place, the Swift Creek Baptist Church, the Mill Pond Restaurant, and the Boykin Mill, is listed on the National Register of Historic Places. Groups are welcome and tours are available.

In the ***Boykin Mill General Store,*** 81 Boykin Mill Road, Rembert 29128, you can get breakfast or a light lunch and then sit out on the porch and watch the road. Almost nothing comes along but an occasional slow-moving dog or an even slower-moving buzzard. The store, with wooden shelves to the high ceiling, sells, among other goods, Boykin's Unsalted Water Ground Grits; stick candy; and raspberry, wild blackberry, and buttered maple syrups. If you want a bologna sandwich, Alice Boykin can take care of it.

Alice or her mother, Alice, or any of the Boykins that are around will be glad to take you on a tour of the 100-year-old mill a few yards away. You'll see grits and meal ground the way they've been ground down here, by water power on hand-dressed mill stones, for more than 200 years. Cornmeal, for the record, is finely ground grits. When you see and feel the oil in the fresh grits made here, you'll realize that what you haul down from the supermarket shelves is not only a sin but a true tragedy. The General Store is open 9:00 A.M. to 6:00 P.M. Call (803) 424–4731.

Located at 84 Boykin Mill Road, Rembert 29128, the ***Mill Pond Restaurant,*** one of the very best restaurants in the state, is made up of three buildings, all on the National Register. The building on the left is an elaborate kitchen; the one in the middle is a small dining room with an old-fashioned marble fountain counter serving as a bar; and the one on the right is the main dining room, overlooking the very picturesque millpond, which feeds the mill a couple hundred feet away.

A quick glance at the comments left by guests in the guest book will give you a rough idea of the quality of the food here. From Columbia we hear, "First time—no doggie bag." From Charleston, "Slow but good." From Greenville, "Hard as hell to find but worth it." From Chester, "Ya'll need sweet tea." And finally from Darlington, "Yeeeee-haw!" It's even better than that. Open 5:00 to 10:00 P.M. Tuesday, Wednesday, and Saturday, and 5:00 to 11:00 P.M. Friday and Saturday. Call (803) 424–0261.

Quail hunters of the world should know that Boykin is the home of the Boykin Spaniel. Right here is where the Boykin family bred the dog, trained it, and introduced it to the hunting world. For further information on this, you can call the Boykin Spaniel Society at (803) 425–1032.

South Carolina not only leads the nation in poisonous snakes—we have seven kinds—it's also up there in the top ten list of fast-food stores per square mile. If you stay on the main roads you'll see them lined up cheek-by-jowl, and if you're downwind the grease is so thick you'll have to use your wipers. So stay on the back roads as much as possible—back where they paint ARE YOU READY FOR JESUS? on the rocks and the automobile tires swing in the chinaberry trees.

Route 261 out of Boykin, heading back toward Camden, is a back road. Turn right at Route 521 toward Sumter and 10 or so miles down the road is Rembert, the home of **Lilfred's,** one of the very best restaurants in the Carolinas and Georgia, located at 11 Main Street, Rembert 29128. When you're this far off the beaten path, you have to be good to attract the crowd they have been attracting for the past forty-odd years. People come here from everywhere. And they keep coming back. Some of their specialties are rib-eye steak, free-range chicken, oysters Rembert, and onion rings. Prices are $15 to $35 for dinner. It's worth it. It's open 6:00 to 9:30 P.M., Wednesday through Saturday. If you're in the mood to write them the address is P.O. Box 205, Camden 29020, or call (803) 432–7063.

South of Rembert on Route 521 you'll come to Sumter, the home of **Shaw Field Air Force Base** on Highway 378. Many of the attack planes that were used in Desert Storm came from here. When you drive by you can see them out on the ramps, shooting landings and take-offs. This restricted base is usually not open to the public, but with advance notice (two weeks minimum) tours can be arranged for groups of twelve or more. Children must be older than thirteen. For more information call (803) 895–2019.

Ward's Barbecue, at 416 East Liberty Street, Sumter 29153 (803–775–2490), is open only on Thursday, Friday, and Saturday from 10:30 A.M. to 7:30 P.M. They are closed Sunday and Monday and cooking is done on Wednesday. Eating barbecue down here is usually done on the weekends, so most barbecue places follow this schedule. At Ward's you can have a barbecue sandwich with a side of coleslaw for $2.75. Soft drinks are available in the vending machine outside. You sit outside on cement chairs at a cement table and watch the trains go by. If you like corn dodgers, which are the same as hush puppies, they are available at $1.50 per dozen.

At the other end of Liberty Street is **Swan Lake Iris Gardens,** which is one of the most attractive and best-run free city parks in the state. One-hundred-foot-high leaf pine and cypress trees surround the fifty-acre lake. Be sure to take a long look at the cypress knees sticking up from the water—this is how the tree breathes. Out on the lake are six different kinds of swans from all over the world, along with ducks, geese, and heron. May is the big season for the Iris Festival. This is when the six million Japanese iris planted here come into bloom. Azaleas, camellias, and roses also bloom in profusion. An old fire engine is available for kids to climb on, under, and over, which they do by the hour. Call the Sumter Chamber of Commerce at (803) 775–1231 for more information on festival dates.

Big Jim's at 451 Broad Street, Sumter 29150, in the heart of town is a landmark in Sumter. With five private dining rooms, a tavern, and a very fine coffee shop, it stays busy. The buffet lunch is especially good at $5.15. Seafood dinners start at $14, and lobsters are available. For reservations call (803) 773–3343.

Due south of Sumter on Highway 6 is **Santee State Park.** This immense tract of land is devoted to fishing, camping, hiking, horseback riding, and golf on the shores of Lake Marion, one of the biggest lakes in the state. Once again, since this is a nonprofit state park, the prices for lodging, golf,

Bombing and Strafing

*H*ere's a slam dunk winner that you will never ever forget. Shaw Field (Airforce Base), located 20 miles south of Columbia at Wedgefield on Route 261, has provided a state-of-the-art showcase like nothing in the entire country. Out on the Poinsett Electronic Combat Range, which features combat planes practicing low-altitude bombing and very low-altitude strafing runs, Shaw Field personnel have erected a set of bleachers for the curi-ous. It's a huge mound with bleachers on top. If you look to the left, you will see the bombing; to the right, the strafing—only 200 yards from where you're sitting. You will also see many of the high-speed planes that fought in Desert Storm. Bring your cameras and ear plugs. This is a real experience, and your kids will love you forever. Since the schedule varies from week to week, call (803) 895–2597 for exact times.

camping, fishing, and so on are very reasonable. For information write Santee State Park, 251 State Park Road, Santee 29142, or call (803) 854–2408.

Due west of Santee on Route 301 and then on Route 4 you'll come to the old railroad town of Springfield, where the tracks run right down Main Street. The *Springfield Frog Jump* is the main event here and is held in October every year. Call (803) 258–3152 for exact dates and information. The owner of the winner of the event and the frog itself—you can raise your own frog, or you can buy one from the local kids—are flown out to Calaveras County, California, for the National Jump-Off. The contest here is staged in the middle of the town. After considerable music and ballyhoo about the history and significance of the frog jump, the contestants are asked to step up on the platform and announce where they are from, whom they are related to, and what their frog's name is. Following this the dignitaries lead the contestants and their frogs out to the launching pad. Old-timers in their nineties and children barely out of their mother's arms can and do enter the contest. The frogs' names run the gamut from Flash to Captain Marvel to Spiro Agnew to Desert Storm. The method of operation is simple: The frog takes three jumps and the overall length is measured. One enterprising contestant with his eye on the California jump-off introduced his frog to a nonlethal snake at the last second before launching, hoping to scare it into a greater jump. This proved disastrous. The frog froze, relieved himself, and had to be taken away, still staring out into the middle distance; it recovered later and jumped in the consolation trials. The Carolina record is an 18-foot jump, but for the past twenty years most of the Calaveras County, California, winners have been from the West Coast.

Due east about 20 miles from Springfield on Route 4 is Aiken, which is best known for its thoroughbred horses, its polo teams, and the *Willcox Inn* at 100 Colleton Avenue, Aiken 29801 (803–649–1377). In the inn's lobby you'll see the two huge stone fireplaces in front of which Franklin Roosevelt and Winston Churchill sat during World War II watching the fire, drinking brandy, and wondering what their next move should be.

The *Aiken County Historical Museum* at 433 Newberry Street, Aiken 29801, is an enormous 14,000-square-foot house built to display a series of rooms furnished in turn-of-the-century style. It also displays agricultural equipment and old firefighting units and has a natural-history room. It is open Tuesday through Friday from 9:30 A.M. to 4:30 P.M. and Saturday and Sunday from 2:00 to 5:00 P.M. Admission is free. Call (803) 642–2015.

Healing Springs

*I*f you have given up on the medical
profession and over-the-counter med-
ication and are suffering from back-
aches, legaches, and head-, shoulder-
and footaches, there is still hope. It's not
only cheap, it's free. All you have to do is
get there. And the trip is very, very
pleasant. From Columbia take SC 302
south to U.S. 178 and turn left. Continue on 178 until you hit SC 3. Turn
right on Healing Springs Road—
clearly marked. Turn right again on
Healing Springs Court. If you see cows
in a field, you've gone too far. Back up
until you see the stream and twelve
spouts that never stop running. This is
it!

The hard fact is that every month,
thousands of people venture down
these very same roads to Healing
Springs to wash and drink and carry
home the magical elixir. Some carry
as many as 100 one-gallon milk jugs
filled with it. A test conducted years
ago revealed that city or county water
will turn green and slimy in a jar after
a few months, but the water from
Healing Springs will remain clear.
Legend has it that the Cherokee Indians first discovered it and used it until
one Nathanial Walker purchased it
from a tribal chief for a few bags of
grain. Since then the property has
gone through six owners until 1944,

when the late L. P. Boylston was so
moved by the cures that he deeded the
land and the springs to God, which
allows the springs to remain free to the
public. Boylston's deed reads, "I should
return to God the most treasured piece
of this earth that I have ever owned
and possessed."

Many of the faithful will swear they've
been cured of everthing from lower
back pain to heart conditions, and a
few will take a blood oath and swear
that if people are baptized in the Healing Waters stream or drink from the
twelve spouts that never stop running,
they won't backslide to their former
ways. Fortunately there have been no
sightings of the Virgin Mary or old
Lucifer lurking in the rhododendrums.
Hopefully, since Blackville is truly off
the beaten path, maybe the National
Enquirer will leave it alone. As for me,
I kept my right hand in the stream for
five full minutes, hoping to soften it up
at impact on my tee shots and turn my
hooks into fades.

You can eat a fine meal at a reasonable price at Miller's Bread Basket, 483
Main Street, Blackville 29817. For
more information on the springs and
Miller's Bread Basket, call the
Blackville Town Hall at (803) 284–
2444. This town is so small that everybody knows everybody.

If the **Palmetto Golf Club,** located right in the center of Aiken, isn't the
oldest course in the country, it's close. Twelve identical rocking chairs sit
on the porch overlooking the first tee and eighteenth green—the way
they have been sitting since the clubhouse was built in 1902 by none
other than Evelyn Nesbit's lover, Stanford White. White was also the
man who designed the Shinnecock clubhouse, Madison Square Garden,

and Grand Central Station. The course itself was remodeled by Alister MacKenzie, the same Scotsman who built the Augusta National, Royal Melbourne, and Cypress Point out in California. Many of the pros stop off at Palmetto for a practice round before they play in The Masters, which is right over the Savannah River a few miles away. In the pro shop is a 1984 photograph of Tom Moore, the pro here, giving Ben Crenshaw some spiritual advice on putting. Crenshaw went on to win The Masters that year, and he's been coming back to see Tom Moore and play Palmetto every year since. He won it again in 1995. Palmetto is a private course, but if you know a pro who knows Tom Moore there's always a chance you can play here. If you know someone who knows Ben Crenshaw that would be even better. If you don't golf, this is still a great place to visit. Call (803) 649–2951.

A few miles north of Springfield is the town of Salley, the home of the annual *Chitlin Strut,* which is an extravaganza that would be sinful to miss. And what is a chitlin? A Low Country historian is credited with the immortal line, "A chitlin is better discussed than described." Anatomically, they are the intestines of the hog, which normally are used as sausage casings or ground up into lunch meat and hot dogs. Some folks eat them as a dish in themselves. Some even eat a lot of them and actually enjoy them. The long tube-like affair is stretched out and scraped down, turned inside out and scraped again. Then it is stump whipped. Three lengths are braided together, boiled until tender,

Animal Facts

A mockingbird can and will imitate any sound in the spectrum. It is gray and black with white sergeant stripes on its wings.

Red-tailed hawks will come right down Main Street in any town down here looking for food. If they get hungry enough they will eat a large pigeon.

Hawks will fly upside down (and have been spotted doing so) so they can grab annoying crows from underneath and kill them. They don't eat them; they just kill them and drop them. Weird, right?

If you see a big hound howling at noth-ing in particular, wait thirty to forty seconds and you'll hear the train they've picked up with their fine tuning.

Possums—the small dogs that don't bark—are absolutely harmless. Even in Columbia, Charleston, and Greenville, the three big cities down here, they can often be seen at night on the street carrying their litter on their backs.

During the Depression possums were hunted and cooked and even served. I asked my Dad how they were eaten. He said, "Fast," and changed the subject.

battered, deep-fat fried, and served. At Salley in late November as many as five, six, or seven tons of chitlins are served and eaten. One old-time cook said, "Lord, we'd never cook them things here in the summertime. That smell would kill every green thing growing."

During the "boil down" part of the process no buzzards circle Salley and no jackals stalk the live oaks and the scrub pine. Small dogs whine and cringe, and large ones head for the corn and bean rows to escape the suffocating stench that hangs in the air—impenetrable, insoluble, incredible. An outsider once moaned, "How do ya'll stand it?" The cook answered, "You get so you get used to it. Go sit in the car and turn the air conditioner on. You don't look so good."

During the "Strut" the town is packed with ten to twenty thousand people all lined up for the hot, greasy fare. They eat and drink beer and lemonade all day and ignore the politicians. Then they hang around for the parade, the beauty pageant, and the high point of the night, "The Chitlin Strut Dance Contest." One heavyset dancer I watched one year introduced himself to the crowd as he came shimmy-walking down the center aisle. When he got to the stage he vaulted over the plastic rhododendron and whipped off an epileptic mountain clog dance that stopped just short of a serious seizure and put the judges in his pocket. Then, swishing his generous hips from side to side, he grinned over his shoulder at the screaming crowd and established one immutable law of "The Chitlin Strut." It is not a thin man's dance. It requires bulk, displacement, a stomach, and a rear view of hips, loins, and other choice cuts that a thin man or woman cannot provide. He won the contest hands down and ruled supreme for four straight years.

As with the frog jump, the day of the "Strut" changes every year, but it's always in late November. Since there are no places to stay in Salley, unless you want to sleep on the ground or in your car, it's best if you get a room in Columbia or over in Aiken. But stay someplace because this is something you'll never, ever forget. Bring your camera. Like the old cook says, "Man, all we have is fun down in here." For information phone (803) 258–3485.

OFF THE BEATEN PATH

Places to Stay in The Fall Line

BENNETTSVILLE
Breeden House Inn
404 East Main
Bennettsville 29512
(843) 479–3665

CAMDEN
Candlelight Inn
1904 Broad Street
Camden 29020
(803) 424–1057

Greenleaf Inn
1308 North Broad Street
Camden 29020
(803) 425–1806

Places to Eat in The Fall Line

CAMDEN
Old South Restaurant
402 De Kalb Street
Camden 29020
(803) 713–0009

REMBERT
Boykin Mill General Store
81 Boykin Mill Road
Rembert 29128
(803) 424–4731

Lilfred's Restaurant
8425 Main Street
Rembert 29128
(803) 432–7063

Mill Pond Restaurant
84 Boykin Mill Road
Boykin 29128
(803) 424–0261

WINNSBORO
News & Herald Tavern
114 East Washington Street
Winnsboro 29180
(803) 635–1331

Uplands and Columbia

Blue Ridge Foothills

The land north and west of Aiken changes dramatically from low, flat pastureland to lush foothills of the Blue Ridge Mountains and finally to the mountains themselves, which rise to more than 3,500 feet. East of Aiken are the **J. Strom Thurmond Dam** and the **J. Strom Thurmond Lake.** If this isn't enough Strom Thurmond for you, you can go 20 miles west to Edgefield, where you can see him striding manfully in bronze in the middle of the town square in Edgefield; this is his home. Edgefield is a beautiful town built around a classic courthouse and a small formal square. It has been home to nine South Carolina governors as well as J. Strom Thurmond.

The most famous trial at the courthouse here was the one of Becky Cotton, born in 1780. She killed her first husband by running a mattress needle through his heart; she poisoned her second; and she split the head of her third with an ax. The trial was even more interesting than the murders. While the evidence of her guilt was overwhelming, her beauty was too much for the judge and the jury. Not only was she acquitted, one of the jurymen became her fourth husband.

Later, the author Mason Locke Weems seized on the story for one of his moral pamphlets, "The Devil in Petticoats," or "God's Revenge Against Husband Killing." From his quill we read " . . . Mrs. Cotton came off clear—nay, more than clear—she came off the conqueror. For as she stood at the bar in tears, with cheeks like rosebuds wet with morning dew and rolling her eyes of sapphires, pleading for pity, their subtle glamour seized with ravishment the admiring bar—the stern features of justice were all relaxed, and both judge and jury hanging forward from their seats breathless, were heard to exclaim, 'Heaven! What a charming creature!'"

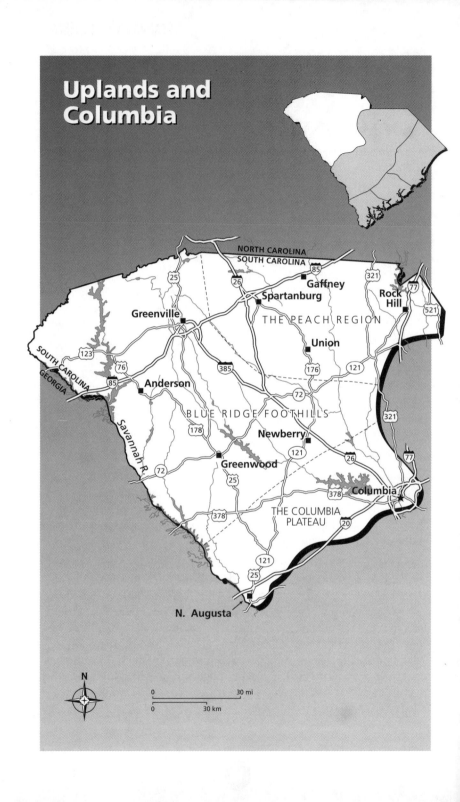

Uplands and Columbia

NORTH CAROLINA
SOUTH CAROLINA

Gaffney

Spartanburg

Rock Hill

Greenville

THE PEACH REGION

Union

SOUTH CAROLINA
GEORGIA

Anderson

BLUE RIDGE FOOTHILLS

Newberry

Greenwood

Columbia

THE COLUMBIA PLATEAU

Savannah R.

N. Augusta

N

0   30 mi
0   30 km

West on Route 23 for a couple miles and then up Route 121 for 40 miles through some very fine pastureland, you'll come to Newberry, home of **Newberry College.** Along with the college you'll find whole blocks of historic buildings dating from the 1800s. The college and many of the homes are listed on the National Register of Historic Places.

On Main Street, right in the heart of the old town, is the **Old Newberry Courthouse,** which is now a community hall. The flamboyant relief on the front of the building—an eagle with a palmetto tree in its clutches—symbolizes the federal government's hold on South Carolina during Reconstruction. For further information about the history here and a tour of Newberry College, go to the Newberry Chamber of Commerce at 1109 Main Street, Newberry 29108, or call (803) 276–4274.

Just down the street is Newberry's pride and joy and reason for celebrating—**The Newberry Opera House.** It was originally built in 1882 but over the years it had deteriorated to the point where it had to be closed. After an extensive renovation, costing more than four million dollars, it had a gala opening with the South Carolina Philharmonic performing Beethoven, Bach, and Handel as well as George Gershwin.

Old Newberry Courthouse

Camelia Johnson and Kevin Maynor of the Metropolitan Opera were also on stage as well as Hal Holbrook and Dixie Carter. The house has 426 seats and in the past has hosted everyone from Lionel Barrymore to cowboy acts. Nicholas Smith, conductor of the philharmonic, and one of the planners for upcoming events—which will range from opera to "opry"—is very excited about the future. "There's no question, it's going to work; of course it's going to work. There's too much good will, good feelings, good effort for it not to."

Two years ago much of downtown was crumbling and on the verge of falling down. But with the renovated opera house, the centerpiece, the old town has come back to life. Art galleries, antique shops, and restaurants now line the once deserted streets and, what is even more

AUTHOR'S FAVORITE PLACES

Cafe and Then Some
(Greenville)

Chatooga River

*South Carolina
State Museum*
(Columbia)

Trustus Theatre
(Columbia)

*Riverbanks
Zoological Park*
(Columbia)

Goatfeathers
(Columbia)

important, above the stores people are already moving into apartments. For tickets or more information write Opera House, Box 357 Newberry 29108, or call (803) 276–5179.

Five minutes out Mendenhall Road from downtown Newberry is the **Carter and Holmes Nursery,** where you can see some of the finest orchids in the Southeast on display and for sale. There is no admission charge, and the range and variety of orchids in the greenhouses is nothing less than stunning. Open from 8:00 A.M. to 4:00 P.M. Monday through Saturday. Call (803) 276–0579.

Dining is best done 7 or 8 miles away down Route 17 in Prosperity at the **Back Porch.** I had the barbecued chicken (excellent), green beans, corn and coleslaw, corn bread, and a pitcher of iced tea all for the whopping price of $4.20. Then I went next door to the **Back Porch Bakery,** bought a lemon cookie the size of a manhole cover for 45 cents, and then strolled up and down Main Street eating it. Then I went back to the bakery, bought a dozen cookies, a loaf of banana bread, and five slices of red velvet cake and got back on the road. The bakery also sells jams, jellies, and red raspberry preserves. A couple of days later I learned that people drive 30 and 40 miles to eat lunch and dinner here. I can see why. Open Tuesday through Saturday from 11:00 A.M. to 8:00 P.M. and Sundays from 11:00 A.M. to 2:00 P.M. Closed Mondays. Call (803) 364–3556.

South of Newberry on Route 121, turn right on Route 34 and go about 24 miles to Greenwood, the home of **Park Seed Company,** which is the largest and oldest family-owned mail-order seed company in America. Located at Cokesbury Road and Highway 254, Greenwood 29647 (864–223–8555), the garden shop and the enormous greenhouses are open from 9:30 A.M. to 6:00 P.M. Monday through Saturday. The best times to visit here are in the spring and during the Festival of Flowers Show in July. More than 70,000 plants are planted in the trial gardens here and can be seen all year round.

Twelve miles west of Greenwood and perched on a series of small hills is my favorite small town, Abbeville. Centered around a good-sized square and dominated by the tall, thin spire of Trinity Church, the old low-skyline town looks as if it has been here forever. Much work has gone into the preservation of downtown. Everywhere you look, from the hardware store to the drugstore to the poolroom to the Opera House, you realize this is exactly the way the old town was built and it's exactly the way people here are going to make sure it stays. This is a joy to see.

The most prominent building here is the **Belmont Inn,** a Spanish-style hotel built in the 1800s. It originally housed travelers and the performers appearing next door at the **Abbeville Opera House.** The hotel went into a decline in the 1920s, and for a long time it stood unused. Finally, in the 1980s, at the insistence of a very active preservation group here in town, the hotel was renovated and reopened. Today, with its period furniture, elegant rooms, and marvelous restaurant, it once again echoes much of the glory of the old Belmont. Today it has air-conditioning. The dining room, called the Heritage Room, serves Continental cuisine. Everything here is excellent. The room is open for breakfast, lunch, and dinner. Dinner rates run between $15 and $25; the desserts are exceptional. You might want to write the Belmont Inn at 106 Court Square, Abbeville 29620, or call (864) 459–9625 and find out the performance schedule for the Opera House. Then book a room around your favorite play or musical. Rates for rooms are from $59 to $159 per night.

The Abbeville Opera House, next door to the Belmont Inn, doesn't have a bad seat in the place and is absolutely stunning. If you're just passing through town and seeing a show is not possible, just stop and stick your head in. You'll be amazed at the size of the enormous stage and the beautiful construction of the balcony. This is probably one of the best designed theaters in the country, and the Abbevillians take great pride in bringing first-class productions to it year in and year out. The acting and directing talent comes from all over the Southeast, but much of it is from right here in Abbeville County. For reservations and a theater schedule, call the Opera House at (864) 459–2157.

Beautiful hills, lakes, and horse and cattle country lie northwest of Abbeville as the land rises into the foothills of the Blue Ridge Mountains. But, frankly, there isn't much to do but look at it. The best stop between Abbeville and Clemson is the town of Pendleton. And the best stop here is the bed-and-breakfast **Liberty Hall Inn** at 621 South Mechanic Street, Pendleton 29670. This is a 150-year-old family house that has been rebuilt and restored and is now one of the best bed-and-breakfasts in the state. The rooms are large, with high ceilings and heart pine floorboards. They are furnished in antiques. Each room has air-conditioning, a telephone, a television, and a private bath. Local arts and crafts from the town and nearby Clemson University are displayed throughout the inn, and much of that artwork is for sale. Incidentally,

Football Mania
(Clemson Tigers)

Coon Williams, a local scribe, once said, "Some anthropologists maintain that Clemson tailgating is a cultural event compara-ble to the 'Chitlin Strut' and the 'Springfield Frog Jump.' But I say there is nothing out there on the boards as outrageous as 80,000 Clemson fans shrink-wrapped in orange (the school color) eating and drinking, listening to taped highlights of the '81 season (the year they won the National Championship), and their 'Tiger Rag' auto horns blaring and standing in line for the Port-O-Johns—and that's why I love them." Here ends the chronicle.

the staff all seem to be college students, which gives this unique inn an even nicer touch. Rates are $85 to $89 per night with a Continental breakfast. If you're not staying here, you can always eat here. Dinner is served from 5:30 to 8:30 P.M. Thursday through Saturday. Lunch is served from 11:30 A.M. to 2:00 P.M. Tuesday through Fri-day. Prices are $15 to $25. The wine list is impres-sive, and other spirits are, of course, available. Call (864) 646–7500. Don't try to stay here during the football season—it's booked solid.

Right in the middle of Pendleton, which is a stun-ning town, is the *Farmer's Hall Restaurant* at 105 Exchange Street, Pendelton 29670. The restaurant is in the old courthouse in the center of the square. If you don't have time for dinner here, at least have a glass of wine or a cup of coffee and look over the town from your table under a big oak tree. Prices for lunch are around $4.00 to $7.00; for dinner you'll pay $12.00 to $25.00. Open from 11:30 A.M. to 2:30 P.M. for lunch Monday through Saturday; dinner starts at 5:30 P.M. Mon-day through Saturday. Closed Sunday. Call (864) 646–7024.

While you're in the Pendleton area you're too close to Clemson not to drive through and look over the Clemson University campus, which fea-tures great red-brick buildings, rolling hills, and beautiful trees. The school is famous for textile engineering, architecture, and the liberal arts, and many of its graduates are employed by the big international firms in Greenville and Spartanburg a few miles away. Clemson is also famous for its football, basketball, soccer, and baseball teams.

As a matter of fact you'll need some luck if you want to see a football game. Despite the fact that the stadium seats 80,000, seats are sold out years in advance. But for the dedicated there is a way. Don't go to the sta-dium; go to the *Esso Club* and just stand around—something will hap-pen. It could be a fight, someone might pass out, or die . . . as I said, something. But hang around long enough and you'll get a ticket.

Thirty miles northeast of Pendleton is the tiny crossroads town of Salem. The best way here is up Route 11, but you'll have to watch for the signs. A mile out of town on a high-rising hill—you are now in the high foothills of the Blue Ridge Mountains—is the *Sunrise Farm Bed and*

Breakfast Inn at 325 Sunrise Drive, Salem 29676. The guest rooms are nicely appointed with period antiques, thick comforters, and family heirlooms. Large windows provide wonderful views of the mountains. This area is famous for hiking and water rafting on the nearby Chattooga. Rates run from $85 to $120 per night, including breakfast. For reservations and further information call (864) 944–0121.

On the shores of Lake Jocassee, which many consider the most beautiful lake in the state, is *Devils Fork State Park* at 161 Holcombe Circle, Salem 29676. Built in cooperation with Duke Power Company, it is managed by the Division of State Parks. Twenty luxurious mountain villas, fifty-nine campsites, swimming facilities, boat ramps, and picnic areas are available. For more information and reservations, call (864) 944–2639.

From Salem a nice trip would be northeast to Sassafras Mountain, which is 3,560 feet and the highest point in South Carolina. This is a

Tigers vs. Gamecocks

Youd need a phone book–thick volume and a ten-hour miniseries to even touch the lore, the action, and the downright insanity of college football down here. First of all, the number one game—and it's the day the state shuts down—is between the Clemson Tigers and the University of South Carolina Gamecocks—a game that goes back to the beginning of time. Tickets are impossible to get. Many are passed on in wills, others are divided up during divorces and right over the graves at funerals, while others are bought on the open market for the price you'd pay for a good used car.

Most people don't even try to get tickets. Some arrive at Clemson Stadium and park their Winnebago near the walls, open their chaise lounges, plug in their TV sets, and turn on the radio. Radio announcers are not only much better down here than TV announcers,

they know the players and their families and if pushed can come up with exactly where they live and the name of their dogs. The spokesman for one group who had gathered at Clemson put everything in perspective. "Friend, what if we got four sets of tickets—which we won't anyhow—but say we did just for argument's sake. First of all we'd have to split up, and we don't want to do that. We've been together for twelve years now. This way we stay together, we don't have to fight the crowd, we can drink all the beer we want, and the john's right here. Hell, all our friends know we're here, and they all come by for some barbecue and pimento cheese. And I'll tell you something else. When the Tigers score and that noise goes up and the old stadium starts rocking, I wouldn't trade this spot for eight box seats with the Board of Trustees."

Trivia

At the Greenville welcome center, there is a water tower painted to resemble a baseball in remembrance of ballplayer Shoeless Joe Jackson of the 1919 Black Sox.

wild and beautiful part of the state, and some of the vistas out over the mountains and valleys look a great deal like Scotland. Driving here at night you'll be amazed how bright the stars are. You'll also be surprised by how few lights you see.

Not too many years ago, the citizens of Greenville decided they weren't going to allow the shopping malls to turn their downtown into a ghost town as they were doing in so many cities across the country. They drew up plans and went to work. Today Greenville's Main Street is a model that other cities facing this same crisis should study. Fine restaurants, dinner theaters, coffeehouses with live music, and wonderfully stocked bars are everywhere, while out on the sidewalk, under a forest of trees, comfortable wooden benches have been arranged into conversation areas where people actually talk to one another. Not only have the citizens of Greenville saved their downtown from the sterilized mall, they have made it into something vastly superior.

The **Cafe and Then Some** is a dinner-theater wonder located at 101 College Street, Greenville 29601 (864–232–2287). Owned and operated by Bill and Susan Smith, this Greenville landmark should not be missed. When asked how business was, Susan, who is also a writer, a singer, and an actress as well as the head cook here, grinned and said, "We ain't got run off yet."

Her menu reads, "Bubba's Rib Eye Steak $16.95 . . . Scientifically designed to arrest any appetite worked up from a busy day of laying around the double wide."

Susan's main claim to fame is her highly successful and very funny play, **Norma Jean and Bubba,** which she not only wrote but stars in and sings in from time to time. In a recent interview to the press she let her hair down. "See, the trick to being a country and western star, which I am, is that your humble origins be more humble than the ones that's already made it big. So I will be sure to tell you that I came from dirt, dirt, dirt, dirt. Upstate red clay, mill village dirt."

Cafe and Then Some is open Wednesday through Saturday. Dinner is served from 6:30 to 7:30 P.M. Shows start at 8:30 P.M. If you can't make it for dinner and you can't make it for the show, at least go by and say hello to Susan and Bill. After a couple minutes with them you'll see why downtown Greenville is not only alive and well but absolutely thriving. Call (864) 232–2287.

Another landmark in Greenville is *The Clock Drive-In* at 1844 Wade Hampton Boulevard, Greenville 29609. Curb boys actually come out to the car, take your order, and bring it back to you the way they have been doing for the past forty years or so. Everything is good here, especially the barbecue and the onion rings, and everything is modestly priced. No matter what you eat, it will be hard spending more than $6.00. Open from 9:30 A.M. to 11:00 P.M. Monday through Thursday; noon to midnight on Friday and Saturday; and 9:30 A.M. to 10:30 P.M. Sunday. Closed only on Christmas and Thanksgiving. For even faster service, which is hard to imagine, call (864) 244–5122.

While you're at the Clock you might as well go a block to the left and through the gates of Bob Jones University. This is the largest non-denominational Christian liberal arts university in the world. This is also the high-water mark of fundamentalism, which ranges across everything from the long skirts the girls must wear to the neckties on the boys, from the heavily censored library to the campus bookstore, which looks a lot like the gift and book shop of Tammy Faye Bakker back when Heritage U.S.A. down the road was booming. I've written two books of short stories and three novels and I'm a South Carolina native living only 100 miles away—none of my books made the cut. Of course, neither did Pat Conroy, James Dickey, or Josephine Humphries (all South Carolinians), nor did J. D. Salinger, Norman Mailer, Joan Didion, Kurt Vonnegut, or Gabriel Garcia Marquez.

Despite all this, Bob Jones University—F. Lee Bailey went to school here—is worth a visit. *The Bob Jones University Museum & Gallery* displays thirty galleries of European sacred art from the thirteenth through the fourteenth centuries and includes important works of many major artists, such as Rembrandt, Tintoretto, Titian, Veronese, Sebastino del Piombo, Cranach, Gerald David, Murillo, Rivera, Rubens, Van Dyck, Honthorst, and Dore. Unfortunately the majority of the paintings are of Jesus's last agonizing moments on the cross—it might be wise to keep the small kids away. One-hour guided tours are available to groups of ten to fifty by reservation only. Call (864) 242–5100, extension 1015. The museum is open Tuesday through Sunday from 2:00 to 5:00 P.M. Admission is $5.00 for adults, $4.00 for senior citizens, $3.00 for students with ID, and free for kids ages six to twelve if accompanied by an adult.

In keeping with Bob Jones's strict rules of how we should conduct ourselves, women are not allowed into these rooms wearing shorts or tight pants! I'm glad they didn't see my tattoos.

The Peach Region

Until twenty years ago the midlands area was largely supported by textile mills, cotton, soybeans, tobacco, and a huge peach crop. Recently this has all been changing, and we now see a growing industrial revolution culminating in the opening of a new giant BMW plant.

Spartanburg, with an elevation of about 900 feet, is in the foothills of the Blue Ridge Mountains. The county and the city get their name from the Spartan Regiment, a body of South Carolina militia that was formed in this area and served with distinction during the Revolution. Its most noteworthy engagement was at Cowpens, in what was one of the decisive battles of the war.

Today Spartanburg is a surprisingly cosmopolitan city. It has even taken on an international quality. A good example of this change is the very fine **Gerhard's Cafe** at 1200 East Main Street, right on the town square. They feature a menu of German and Austrian entrees as well as pastas, duck, rack of lamb, and pepper steak. Prices are from $15 to $28. Open for dinner Monday through Saturday. Call (864) 591-1920.

Seven blocks away on Church Street, with a high hilltop setting of sixty-five acres or so, are the beautiful old, red-brick buildings of **Wofford College,** founded in 1850 and governed by the Methodist Church of South Carolina. The school is internationally known for its program in the liberal arts, especially in English and history. On the campus is a simple granite monument over the graves of Doctor Benjamin Wofford, the founder, and his wife, Anna Todd. The monument bears the same Latin inscription as the grave of Sir Christopher Wren, translated as IF YOU WOULD SEE THIS MONUMENT, LOOK ABOUT YOU.

As you drive northwest from Spartanburg on I-85 the kids will spot the big peach first. It's an enormous one-million-gallon water tower painted like a ripe peach, and it's meant to tell you you're getting close to Gaffney, the home of the **Gaffney Peach Festival.** This is peach country—as a matter of cold fact, Spartanburg and Cherokee counties produce more peaches than all of Georgia. Gaffney, a town of 13,600, is not only the home of The Peach Festival, which is in the first week of July and attracts as many as 300,000, but also of **Limestone College,** the state's oldest institution of higher education for women. It's also the site of at least a dozen National Register homes that date back to the early 1800s.

Here's a little background on Gaffney. Back in 1835 promoters took over the town and ballyhooed it as the South's Saratoga. This was the heyday of therapeutic mineral treatment, and plantation owners from Charleston

Peach water tower, Gaffney

and the Low Country, plagued every summer by malaria, flocked here to drink the water, gamble in the casino, and visit the racetrack. Gaffney also became famous for its jousting tournaments, cockfights, and gander pullings (which is the fine but mercifully lost art of snatching off the head of a plucked and greased goose while riding at a hard gallop).

After this medicine-show enterprise failed, Gaffney evolved into a thriving textile mill center until the mill closings of the last thirty years. Today, four mills are still here, employing about 2,000 workers, and the Nestlé Frozen Food Company and Timken Roller Bearing Company also operate here, but downtown Gaffney has been neglected and allowed to go to seed. One can hope that one day they will follow Greenville's lead and renovate a few of the old buildings, plant some trees, and bring the old town back to life, but in the meantime this is still a good stopover because you can see the beautiful buildings of Limestone and the old homes.

If you want to find the perfect place to get an idea of how an old mill town must have felt not too many years ago, go to *Harold's Restaurant* in the heart of downtown Gaffney. It has a four-table poolroom and bar next door, and it does a thriving lunch and short-order business, with prices right out of the 1960s. A chicken salad sandwich, which is very good, is only $1.00; a pint of coleslaw is only $1.50. During the Peach Festival people line up for the take-out specials—a pint of chicken salad at $3.50, a gallon of chili for $18.00. Reservations aren't needed, but if you want to order over the phone and then pick it up, call (864) 489–9153. The new owner, Tony Lipscomb, is very young and very personable and will be glad to tell you about Gaffney and the Peach Festival.

Back on I–85 you will see the entrance to Route 11, also called *Cherokee Foothills Scenic Highway.* If you can spare the time, this beautiful 130-mile road through the heart of the state's Blue Ridge Mountains will take you back to I–85 on the other side of the state. The following are a few of the incredible vistas along the way.

Caesar's Head has been a resort since antebellum times. It features a rock that juts out from the mountainside more than 1,200 feet above the Saluda River valley. Literature and exhibits are available at the visitor's center here that describe the natural history of the area, with particular emphasis on the trails systems and the history of the early settlers of the area. Call (864) 836–6115.

Raven Cliff Falls, located off Route 276 near Greenville county, is a 420-foot-high cascade in the Mountain Bridge Wilderness and Recreation Area and is one of the most breathtaking waterfalls in South Carolina. A 2-mile hike is necessary to reach the area.

Sassafras Mountain, which stands 3,554 feet high, is the highest point in South Carolina. From the top, four states can be viewed: Tennessee, North Carolina, South Carolina, and Georgia.

The *Chattooga National Wild and Scenic River,* another highlight of the Cherokee Foothills Scenic Highway, is a mecca for whitewater enthusiasts.

Chattooga River Adventures off Route 76 at Mountain Rest offers canoe and kayak instruction and rents rafts, canoes, and kayaks. Guided whitewater tours are available and can easily be arranged. Call (800) 647–0365. Lodging is also available here. *Wildwater, Ltd.* proudly announces that they have safely carried more than 300,000 guests on their half-day, full-day, and two-day trips on the Chattooga. Trips on Section 3 of the Chattooga are perfect for families and youth groups. Section 4 is for the more advanced and more adventuresome. Call (864) 647–9587.

From Gaffney due east on Routes 29 and 5 the next stop is York, which was settled by the Scots and the Irish in the 1700s. For a time in the 1920s and 1930s the Barnett Brothers' Circus made its winter quarters here. Back then every Christmas the shopping season was officially opened with a parade in which Santa Claus, escorted by the high school band, came swaying down Congress Street perched high above the crowd on the back of an elephant. Even today, it's said a few of the milky-white dogs of the town are descended from the long line of somersaulting terriers of the old circus.

In any event, York is a unique and charming town. The *McCelvey Center,* a 580-seat performing arts theater, is the centerpiece of the community's cultural activities. *Summerfest,* a daylong extravaganza of children's activities, craft fairs, a classic car show, and a fireworks display, is held here on the fourth Saturday in August. It has been designated as one of the top twenty events in the entire Southeast. During the second weekend in December the town hosts *Christmas in Olde York,* when the historic houses, of which there are many, are open to visitors, and the quaint streets are lit by luminarias for candlelight tours.

York is full of surprises, and one is the *Museum of York County,* a few miles east off Route 161 at 4621 Mount Gallant Road, Rock Hill 29732. Watch for the museum signs—they'll lead you right there to the place. The museum features the world's largest collection of mounted African hoofed animals, which are displayed in huge dioramas. My favorite is the rampaging elephant, which is rearing up at least 20 feet and swinging its tusks to the sky. Small kids go wild with this one. The museum also has a planetarium and a nature trail. Admission is $2.00 for adults, $1.00 for children. Open from 9:00 A.M. to 5:00 P.M. daily and Sunday from 1:00 to 5:00 P.M.; closed for major holidays. Call (803) 329–2121.

A few miles south of York on Route 1, visit *Brattonville.* This is a restored village of eighteenth- and nineteenth-century structures erected by several generations of the Bratton family. The homes are furnished with many Bratton pieces, including such items as an old-time biscuit press and a tin bath. One of the structures is a replica of a 1750 dirt-floored backwoodsman's cabin, complete with furniture and kitchen utensils. This restoration is open only on Tuesday, Thursday, and Sunday. Call (803) 684–2327 before you go because the schedule is subject to change. On the other hand, if you get there and everything is closed, you can always walk around the grounds and peer in through the windows. Admission is $4.00 for adults from out of the country (strange), $2.00 for adults who live in the country, and $1.00 for students age eighteen and under.

Nearby Rock Hill is a relatively large town with a population of 40,000. Also settled by Scots and Irish, Rock Hill's name came from the hard rock the railroaders had to deal with when they were laying tracks. Perhaps the most prestigious attraction here is the beautiful designed and wonderfully situated *Winthrop College.* The lush campus, spread out under magnificent oaks and magnolias, is so pleasant you'll want to stroll into every corner of it. Be sure to do so—everybody does. While you stroll, note the *Little Chapel,* the building where the school started. Designed and built by American's first architect, Robert Mills, The Little Chapel originally was in Columbia. In 1936 it was moved here brick by brick. Mills later went on to Washington to design and help build the Washington Monument.

Rock Hill has a new formal entrance called **The Gateway,** which looks as if it should be guarding Lenin's tomb on Red Square or in storage at Universal Studios for use in a Roman epic movie. Two 60-foot Egyptian pillars and four 13-foot bronze statues have been artistically arranged around a circular plaza on David Lyles Boulevard—the effect is one of painful solemnity. New York sculptor Audrey Flack has created the four identical statues of muscular maidens, each holding aloft a symbol of Rock Hill's many accomplishments. According to the inscriptions on the statues' stone bases, the fire is symbolic of the flame of knowledge; the circle of stars represents the city's attention to culture; the set of gears symbolizes Rock Hill's business growth; and the bolt of lightning points out the role the production of electricity has had in Rock Hill's development. I parked here and read every word on every monument and came away convinced that this was the work of a very, very large committee. The kids will love it, but don't make them write a paper on it.

Paramount's **Carowinds** is a 100-acre water and theme park that straddles the North Carolina–South Carolina state line. Located on Carowinds Boulevard, Fort Mill 29715, the park offers more than forty state-of-the-art rides, shows, and movie-themed experiences for all ages. Just take I–77 to exit 90 at the North Carolina–South Carolina border. The park is just fifteen minutes south of uptown Charlotte, N.C., and 12 miles north of Rock Hill, S.C. More than thirty restaurants and snack stands provide a broad variety of dining choices, and the place is absolutely perfect for kids. They even have a gigantic wave pool. Call (803) 548-5300.

The Columbia Plateau

A
s you approach Columbia on I–77 the red clay rises slightly and begins to flatten out. Wildflowers, crepe myrtle, and even azaleas are planted in the median. And then you see it—the brand-new skyline with the copper dome of the old capitol building in the center. The city is on a wide, flat plateau that was once a plantation owned by one Mr. J. T. Taylor, who went public with the outcry: "They ruined a damn fine plantation and built a sorry-assed town." Probably the most scenic drive into the old city, over the great rivers that meet here, is from the west on Jarvis Klapman Boulevard—a name that doesn't exactly trip too lightly over the tongue. Not too long ago we had a rash of avenues,

bridges, landfills and run-off culverts unfortunately named for politicians who were, and are, still in office. And recently a committee has actually named a wide tree-lined beautiful avenue Colonial Life Boulevard.

But there it is—Columbia. Its gold and silver buildings and its copper dome stand under the reflecting clouds, illuminated like something out of a fairy tale or Disney World or the Land of Oz. The city is a study in contrasts. Out on the fringe you can still find combination general stores and service stations that sell night crawlers, bloodworms, and crickets to the anglers and candy from a curved glass case to the kids. You'll see smoked hams and mule collars along with fan belts and plow points hanging from the ceilings. Out front between the gas pumps will be the slick wooden bench where the old-timers still play checkers with bottle caps and watch the traffic going by.

Against these rustic reminders of the 1930s, the 1940s, and the 1950s, the city claims fifteen-story buildings of steel and colored glass, gourmet restaurants, three ballet companies, and a very fine South Carolina Shakespeare Company that performs for free in the city parks. The airport even offers nonstop air service to New York City and one-stop service to Los Angeles. And, just eight blocks west of the State House—in the center of the city—the Congaree River runs by the State Museum and the brand-new Congaree Vista Park. It's right here in the Congaree that you can, with just a few arrangements, take a crack at catching a striped bass. The record was set early this year—forty-eight pounds. This is something you won't find in too many cities out there in the great Republic.

Columbia is the home of the University of South Carolina, which has grown from an enrollment of 4,000 students in the 1950s to a present-day student body of 25,000 at the campus in the heart of town. USC has a medical school and a law school, and for the past few years the USC School of International Business has been rated among the nation's best by *U.S. News and World Report.*

The city prides itself on the state-of-the-art **Richland County's Main Library,** an architectural masterpiece on four levels, each approximately one acre. This 242,000-square-foot building is one of the largest for an urban community of its size in the Southeast. The beautiful steel and glass construction with wonderful natural lighting and a forest of trees is truly all a library should be. The centerpiece here is the permanent art on the Garden Library, a 40-foot mural 18 feet high depicting the "wild rumpus scene" and two freestanding characters, all from Maurice Sendak's children's classic *Where the Wild Things Are.* This is the

A Very Short History of South Carolina Football

*R*ight smack in the middle of the dog days of September, when the northern transplants are wondering when, and if, the summer will ever end, the madness begins. We break out our Gamecock jackets, caps, and banners, and start politicking for a parking space within 1,000 yards of Williams-Brice Stadium. And then it's Saturday and there we are, where we've been sitting forever, watching Gamecock football. The game goes on and the stouthearted fans, of ten, twenty, thirty—you name it—years cheer and shout, groan and scream all the way into the fourth quarter. And then as if on signal, when we're 14 or 21 or 27 or 36 points behind, they begin silently filing out and looking forward to the next game and the game after that, as they have been doing since the days when Pitchfork Ben Tillman was ravaging the countryside.

Looking down the ninety-year-old Spanish Moss–draped tunnel of Gamecock football, there is one grim and comic statistic that is seldom reported by the local press. Our best year (except 1984) was 1903—seven wins and three losses. But one of the victories was against the Columbia-based YMCA and the other, an 89 to 0 humiliation of the Welsh Neck High School.

But all this changed in 1984, when we won five in a row and were rated up there with the name brands in the Associated Press Poll. I covered the games that year and here are the notes from my journal: "Back in the not-so-long-ago days of '83, '82, '81, and '80,

right about now we'd be three wins and three losses, and we'd be looking forward to basketball and the winter solstice. But this year was different. This was too crazy to believe. We actually had a football team. We'd always had a football team, but this one was winning. We were actually undefeated in five straight games and were right up there on page one of the sports section in The New York Times, The L. A. Times, and The Chicago Tribune. Right up there with Nebraska, Oklahoma, Texas, Ohio State: schools with ball teams that get on national television and go to bowl games. Schools where the old grads die and leave oil wells and skyscrapers and coastlines to the Athletic Department. Serious big time, household names like Michigan, Penn State, Southern Cal, and Notre Dame."

But now we were winning. The fever had hit Columbia and we were twisting and trembling in torment. New and terrible, weird things were happening all over town—we were out of control. Housebreaking and embezzling and brutal crimes dipped twenty to twenty-five points, but freak accidents increased by thirty. Cars were piling into hedges, phone poles, and runoff culverts; others simply left the road as if "The Rapture" was upon them and they could be seen out in the fresh rows of collards and soy beans. But it wasn't "The Rapture" or the fear of a first strike by the Red Menace, poised somewhere down there in the jungles of Guadalajara. It was pure, cold-biscuit-down-in-the-dirt Gamecock Fear. Our next game was with Notre Dame at Notre Dame, and if by some miracle we won, we would have six wins in a row and be among the top three in the country. At the bars, prayer groups, and Tupperware parties you could feel the fear. You could hear it.

"Hell, I'm breaking out in a Gamecock Rash."

"I need four drinks to feel one."

"My teeth feel soft and the back of my hands itch."

And one howling looper at the end of the bar banged on it two times, three times, four. "I've had it. You hear me? I can't go on like this! I'm calling Jim Holderman and I'm telling him to stop the damn season and send me the bill."

Anyhow, we beat Notre Dame, then N.C. State, then Florida State, and were eight in the row with no losses and right up there at Number 2 in the A. P. Poll. We lost the next game to

Navy but then we beat Clemson and went down to the Gator Bowl, where we lost in the last minute to Oklahoma State. The season ended with nine wins and two losses—the best season ever—and now, over sixteen years later we still haven't recovered. And may never recover. Even today you can see garnet and black bumper stickers pleading and screaming, "WAIT TILL 84!"

And why am I telling you all this? I'll tell you why. For the past 30 or 40 years it has been impossible to get Gamecock tickets. But now that has changed, for in 1998 we started a losing streak of 21 games, which has probably broken every college record on the books. And for the first time in a long, long time tickets are available. So call the Athletic Department at (803) 777–4274 for the schedule and tickets, and come on out to Williams-Brice. You'll never ever forget it.

first time Sendak has authorized such use of his work as public art. The work is not only a wonderful background for the children's area but has been so designed and painted to allow the children to touch it. If you're traveling with kids, put the library on top of your list.

The city also has eight theaters, an enormous and beautiful inner-city park, the very successful Philharmonic Society, and the brand new and very fine *Columbia Museum of Art.* Located in the center of town at 1600 Main Street, Columbia 29201, the museum offers one of the better permanent collections of Baroque and Impressionist art in the entire Southeast. Among the artists represented are Monet, Matisse, Renoir, and such regional artists as Elizabeth O'Neill Verner from Charleston and Jasper Johns, who is from the Columbia area. The museum is open Tuesday through Saturday from 10:00 A.M. to 5:00 P.M. and Sunday from 1:00 to 5:00 P.M. On Wednesday the museum is open from 10:00 A.M. to 9:00 P.M. Closed on Monday. Admission is $4.00 for

OFF THE BEATEN PATH

Not So Fast!

One night back in the '60s Satchell Paige, the famous baseball pitcher, was stopped by the police in the middle of Gervais Street for speeding. When the police recognized him, and after he gave them a stack of autographed eight-by-elevens for their friends and families, they formed a motorcade around his big Cadillac and escorted him on across and out onto the highway to Atlanta.

adults, $2.00 for students and senior citizens, and children age five and under get in free. Call (803) 799–2810.

A recent addition to the USC campus and the city is the Koger Center, a remarkable 4,000-seat auditorium with one of the best stages in the country. Even more recent is the completion of a beltway around the entire city that connects three interstates and joins Columbia—via I–77, I–26, and I–20—to Charleston, Greenville, and Charlotte, North Carolina. Only eleven other cities in the nation share this style of highway transportation system. Now you can drive non-stop from Cleveland all the way to Charleston.

Thirty years ago the only ethnic food you could get in the old Columbia was pizza or maybe a Greek salad. Now, owing to the University's growing number of Asian students and the cosmopolitan population of the Army stationed nearby at Fort Jackson, every cuisine from Vietnamese to Turkish to Indian to take-out sushi is available here. The schools have been integrated since the 1960s and are working as smoothly as those anywhere in the United States—they may, in fact, be better than most. And, at a time when whites-only country clubs are still flourishing across the nation, five of Columbia's six clubs are integrated.

The first stop should be the **South Carolina State Museum** at 301 Gervais Street, Columbia 29201. The building is an old cotton mill, and the floors are foot-thick maple, which was needed to support the heavy textile machinery. This state-of-the-art museum has marvelous exhibits about natural history, science, and technology, with hands-on displays for kids. They can light up a laser beam, talk into the whisper dish and hear their voices across the room, and even handle the fossilized teeth of an extinct mastodon. The transportation display has an ancient 1904 Oldsmobile as well as a modern space suit worn by General Charles M. Duke, Jr., an astronaut from South Carolina. Open Monday through Saturday 10:00 A.M. to 5:00 P.M. and Sunday from 1:00 to 5:00 P.M. Adults pay $4.00, children age six through seventeen, $1.50; free for children age five and under. Call (803) 737–4977.

Turning on Gervais Street, you're a block from the Congaree River and some great fishing opportunities anyplace along the bank. To the right, up a block, cross Huger Street and on the right about 40 feet from the corner you'll see a 7 ½-foot red-brick doorway with an arch over the top and no ceiling. Back in the 1940s this was Fox's Fish, the smallest restaurant in town. My grandmother owned it and ran it and sold nothing but fish sandwiches. No beer, no cokes, no iced tea, no pickles. Nothing but a crispy fried fresh fish and two slices of bread for a nickel. The head stuck out one side, the tail out the other. People still talk about how good they were.

On up Gervais another block is *Longhorn Steakhouse,* at 902A Gervais Street, Columbia 29201, which advertises, "No Quiche, No Ferns." Instead they have country music, enough neon for a state fair, and the best steaks in town, with a very good salad for a modest price. This is a big place with many tables and booths. The service is excellent, and the prices are under $15. Call (803) 254–5100.

One of the best but only slightly off-the-beaten path restaurants in the Vista Alley area is *The Motor Supply Company* at 920 Gervais Street. Ten years ago the building that now houses the restaurant was an auto-parts warehouse and store. When the management of the restaurant bought and began renovating the building, they found the old motor supply sign in the basement. It proved so irresistible that not only was the name used but the sign itself now hangs over the main door. Of special interest on the inside is an enormous oak back bar with marble columns that look as if they came out of a Roman bath.

This upscale restaurant features chicken, lamb, veal, steak, and a variety of pasta dishes, and is locally famous for its desserts. They also have a wide range of very good wines. Prices are around $15 for lunch and range from $20 to $25 for dinner. Open for lunch Tuesday through Saturday 11:30 A.M. to 2:30 P.M., dinner is served from 6:00 to 10:00 P.M. Tuesday through Thursday; 6:00 to 11:00 P.M. Friday and Saturday; and 6:00 to 10:00 P.M. Sunday. Closed Monday. Sunday brunch is served from 11:00 A.M. to 3:00 P.M. Sunday night is Thai night, from 5:00 to 11:00 P.M. Call (803) 256–6687 for reservations or just drop in.

A block west of Motor Supply at 804 Gervais is *Adluh Milling Company,* which produces flour, meals, corn-bread mix, and another dozen milled products. Their old red neon has been burning high on the roof over Columbia for as long as most people can remember. Adluh is owned by the Allen brothers, who have made a career out of supporting education in the state through donations and scholarships to colleges and universities. The factory itself offers guided tours for schoolchildren, Scouts, senior citizens, and other groups. Each tour is capped with a visit to their hospitality room, where biscuits or hush puppies are baked right before your eyes, from the flour you just saw made, and served with butter, jams, and jellies. If you'd like to get on one of these tours, which will take you through the mill and show you how flour and the various milled products are made, one of the staff will try to join you up with a group. Call (803) 779–2460.

A few blocks from Adluh Flour is *Miyo's* at 922 South Main, Columbia 29201. This is a very fine restaurant specializing in Shanghai and Szechuan cuisine, located right in the center of the city. Michelle and Yong Wang, both from New York City, moved here a few years ago and have quickly moved into the absolute top spot in the entire county for Chinese cooking. They have a beautiful mahogany bar where they serve hot and chilled sake, liquor, and fine wines. They have recently remodeled and refurnished the old building so that now, along with the delicious food, you can sit in a stunning setting of Oriental art. Hours are Monday through Saturday, lunch 11:30 A.M. to 2:30 P.M. except on Saturday, dinner 5:30 to 10:00 P.M. Prices are $8.00 for lunch, $10.00 to $20.00 for dinner. You can also call ahead for take-out service. Call (803) 779–6496.

Heading back towards Columbia, you must visit *Altman's Wine and Spirits* at 7241 Broad River Road in Irmo. In accordance with the Carolina blue laws, it is open Monday–Wednesday 10:00 A.M. to 7:00 P.M.; Thursday–Saturday 9:00 A.M. to 7:00 P.M. The store has a different concept from most ABC package stores. Instead of the usual traditional dark paneling and mirrored liquor ads on the walls, they have painted the store a light gray, carpeted it in charcoal, and have put in black shelving (virtually unheard of in the industry), which allows you to see the selections very easily. Denise and Jim Altman will even help you plan your wedding, if you just ask! They have a great selection of single-malt scotches, small-batch bourbons, and quality vodkas, but the best part is that you can order any "hard to get" labels of liquors or wines at reasonable prices. (They recommend port, their wine of choice.) Don't forget to ask to be put on their mailing list, because you'll get a full education including histories, recipes, etc., as well as be advised on upcoming drawings, such as their drawing for the world's largest bottle of barbecue sauce! Call (803) 407–9100.

You can't miss the *State House* on the corner of Main and Gervais, Columbia 29201; it's in the center of everything. This blue granite building was shelled by Sherman in 1865 from across the Congaree River. The spots where the shells landed are marked on the western side of the building with bronze stars. On the steps of the capitol is a bronze statue of George Washington, with his cane broken off. The story and the inscription tell us the Union forces "brickbatted it." You can go inside and take the free tour conducted from 9:00 A.M. to noon, and 1:30 to 3:30 P.M. Open Monday through Friday 9:00 A.M. to 4:00 P.M. Call (803) 734–2430.

A block south on Sumter Street just behind the State House is *Town Theater.* While the building is only 100 years old, it has the distinguished record of running continuously for more than eighty-five years. The actors, directors, and stagehands are all local citizens. Call (803) 799–2510 for current schedules.

The *Trustus Theater* at 520 Lady Street, Columbia 29201, is another interesting theater, providing deep comfortable couches as well as soft drinks, beer, and popcorn for the audiences. First-class entertainment and professionally acted and staged plays are always on the playbill here. Call (803) 254–9732 for their current schedule.

Two blocks north of the capitol is the *Equitable Arcade Building* at 1332 Main Street. This amazing and beautiful structure, built in Second Renaissance Revival style in 1912, was Columbia's first enclosed shopping mall. It is now on the National Register of Historic Places. Shaped like an "L" with ornamental facades both on Main Street and around the corner on Washington Street, the two-story Arcade has a central hallway lighted by an enormous skylight. The facing is white terra-cotta marble and decorated ceramic tile. Six huge double-tiered bronze chandeliers provide evening lighting. With all the glass and light and white marble, the old building looks not unlike the gallerias of Florence or Venice. It's a downtown tragedy that the building, probably the most delicate, attractive, and unique structure in the entire city, hasn't been renovated and put to better use. In any event, stop by and walk through. You'll never see anything quite like it again.

Gracie's Tea Room is the brightest bright spot in the old Arcade. Gracie serves wonderful sandwiches, salads, and baked goods. Everything is around $3.00 to $4.00, and you can also take home whole cakes and pies or some of her famous homemade bread. They do a brisk business here and for a very good reason—everything is not only modestly priced but very, very good. Open for lunch Monday through Friday, from 11:30 A.M. to 2:30 P.M. Closed Saturday and Sunday. You can give Gracie's a call at (803) 254–7913.

Richland Street Bed and Breakfast is the perfect place to stay for a quiet weekend in the center of the historic homes district. This newly built house is styled in the grand Victorian manner and furnished accordingly. Rooms run from $89 to $150. A deluxe Continental breakfast and after-

Seibel's House, Columbia

noon refreshments are included in the room rate. The McNair suite ($150) has a sitting room as well as a whirlpool tub and a balcony looking out over the trees and street. All rooms come with rheostat-controlled chandeliers; one room has been specially equipped for handicapped access. A big dining and living room is ideal for relaxing in front of the fire. Call Naomi Perryman for reservations and information at (803) 779–7001.

On the corner of Richland and Pickens, one block from the Richland Street B&B, is *Seibel's House,* the oldest house in Columbia. Built in 1796, it is surrounded by palmetto trees. A separate kitchen built of handmade brick stands behind the house, and there's a large and beautiful garden at the side. Today the house is the headquarters of the Historic Columbia Foundation. While here you can get a free brochure showing the other historic houses in the area as well as maps and information. Open 9:00 A.M. to 5:00 P.M. Monday through Friday. Tours of the house cost $4.00 for adults, $2.50 for students, and children under six are admitted free. Call (803) 252–7742.

Within walking distance from Seibel's House are four National Register homes open for your inspection at no charge. *Hampton-Preston Mansion* at 1615 Blanding, Columbia 29201, is the home of the Wade Hampton family. The first Wade Hampton served in the Revolutionary War and was a general in the War of 1812; Wade Hampton II was an officer in the War of 1812; and Wade Hampton III commanded the Confederate cavalry during the Civil War and later became governor of South Carolina.

Next door is the *Robert Mills House and Park,* at 1616 Blanding Street. Robert Mills is the architect who designed the Washington Monument, the old Patent Office Building, and the United States Treasury Building in our nation's capital. His work is also easily recognizable in buildings all over Columbia.

Mann-Simon Cottage, at 1403 Blanding, was the home of Celia Mann, a slave from Charleston who purchased her freedom with money she earned as a midwife. She walked to Columbia, bought this wooden cottage, and made her home here until her death years later. Today the ground floor is a gallery of artwork where local African-American artists display their art for viewing and purchasing. Books and gifts are available in the gallery.

Woodrow Wilson's Boyhood Home, at 1705 Hampton Street, is adorned with latticework, rose-covered trellises, and a gazebo in the garden. Inside the house are Wilson family pieces, including the bed in which Woodrow Wilson was born. Wilson's father, Joseph Ruggles Wilson, was a Presbyterian minister; he and his wife are buried only a few blocks away at Columbia's First Presbyterian Church, where Reverend Wilson served.

Another two dozen historic sites in Columbia are worth seeing. Among the most notable are ***Tapp's Department Store, Lexington State Bank, Sylvan's Jewelry,*** the ***Governor's Mansion*** on Richland Street, and the ***Lace House*** directly across from it.

Modeled on the open-pit design of the San Diego Zoo, ***Riverbanks Zoological Park*** year after year is rated one of the top ten zoos in the country. Its budget is more than $4 million a year, and it houses more than 2,000 animals in natural settings without cages. In addition, more than 1,000 reptiles, amphibians, and fish from around the world are housed in an aquarian-reptile complex. Located at 500 Wildlife Parkway, Columbia 29201, the Saluda River runs between the zoo and the Botanical Gardens, and the anglers who hear the animal calls at night or in the early morning say it's like being on the Amazon. Kids love the huge seal and sea lion pool, especially at feeding time. Very good outdoor snack bars serve almost anything you like for lunch. If you're one of those people who is going to drive from Cleveland to Charleston on the interstates and you can only make one stop in Columbia, I'd make it the zoo. You can't go wrong: Open daily 9:00 A.M. to 4:00 P.M. Admission is $6.25 for adults (age thirteen and over); $3.75 for children three to twelve; children age two and under admitted free. For further information call (803) 779-8717.

Back on Main Street, six blocks north of the capitol (1734 Main Street, Columbia 29201), stop at ***La Vecchia's Seafood Grille,*** which is more than just a grill where they serve fish. This

"Most Famous Dropout"

My old high school, Columbia High, awarded the "Most Famous Graduate" honor to Cardinal Joseph Bernadin. But coming up hard on the outside track was yours truly with "Most Famous Dropout." Since the Cardinal was too busy with Scriptures to speak at the dedication of the school's new building a few years back, I was chosen. There's a moral here someplace, but I can't put my finger on it.

is a very upscale restaurant with an elaborate wine list and a wonderful menu. While seafood is the main fare here, there is also steak and chicken, and everything is served in a truly different dining atmosphere. The ceiling has been designed and sculpted to resemble the surface of the ocean, and directly above you is a series of metal sculptures of fish ranging from 4 feet long to one enormous one of at least 25 feet. The entire place makes you think you are looking up from the ocean floor. It really has to be seen to be appreciated. They offer at least fifteen varieties of wine that can be ordered by the glass. The bar picks up the undersea motif with a series of fish tanks built into the supporting columns with beautiful yellow and blue tropical fish. There is also outdoor seating for the bar, overlooking the palm trees and young oaks that line Main Street. Altogether, this is a marvelous place to dine. Dinner prices range from $16 to $21. Open 11:30 A.M. to 2:00 P.M. Monday through Friday for lunch, and for dinner 5:30 to 10:00 P.M. Monday through Thursday, 5:30 to 11:00 P.M. Friday and Saturday; closed Sunday. Call (803) 376–8888.

Home of the finest mustard-based, sauce-drenched barbecue in the

A Few More Words about Barbecue

For some reason rednecks down here in the "hard lard belt" are now billing their barbecue as "gourmet barbecue." But it's a free country and you can call it anything you want. Anyhow, there are a few not so well-known facts I thought I'd pass along to the tourists and the transplants to raise their sensitivity and make them much better consumers. Basically there are three classifications for barbecue hogs: the three rib down, the five rib down, and the seven rib down. This is the butcher's term that tells you how much a rack of ribs weighs. What this also tells you is the three rib down comes from a smaller hog that has less fat than the five rib, and considerably less than the seven rib down hog. The result of all this is that the three rib down is smaller and thinner, and has less fat and is obviously tastier. As a result, three ribs down is much more expensive, harder to find, and is really the only truly "gourmet barbecue." A basic rule would be that a buffet of "All You Can Eat Barbecue" that has to withstand the seismic charge of entire football teams will probably be five rib down. Meanwhile, out at the fair and political fund-raising functions where the beer drinkers will eat anything, there is a strong chance it'll be the fatter seven ribs down. I guess it all boils down to this. The next time someone tells you about "gourmet barbecue," ask what kind of hogs he or she uses. They will say, what do you mean? And you answer "Well, judging by the length and weight of this here rib and all this fat dripping on my leisure suit..."

Southeast, **Piggie Park** is so famous its product is shipped to every state in the country and all over the world. Almost as famous is Maurice Bessinger, the owner and operator. During the 1950s he was an ardent segregationist; in the 1960s he found Jesus and became a leading integrationist. Next he ran for governor on a white horse and lost, and then, discovering something in Scripture, he turned his Barbecue Buffeteria into a mission for the gospel.

Today he practices what he preaches; good food at a reasonable price and an unswerving belief in every word of the Scriptures. His dining room is filled with free gospel flyers, but you don't have to take one. But do eat one of his "Little Joe" barbecue sandwiches with a side of the best onion rings you'll ever eat. Back when Al McQuire coached Marquette and they came to town to play USC's Gamecocks, his first stop in town was Maurice's. Joseph Heller, author of *Catch 22*, loves it, and so do Nora Ephron, who directed *Sleepless in Seattle*, and Mickey Spillane, who lives down the road in Murrells Inlet. During Desert Storm the 240th Combat Communications Squadron from nearby McEntire Air Base asked Maurice to send some barbecue to Kuwait. Maurice couldn't fill that order, but when the 200 men returned to Columbia he gave them and their spouses a free all-they-could-eat barbecue meal at the base. Open Monday through Thursday 10:00 A.M. to 11:00 P.M., and Friday and Saturday 10:00 A.M. to midnight. Call (803) 796–0220.

Five Points, a mile or so southeast of the capitol, is the city's main center of activity. Here the university students gather to pound their drums and string their beads. At 2007 Devine, Columbia 29205, right in the heart of Five Points, is **Portfolio Art Gallery.** This is a small but packed-to-the-ceiling store that carries a huge variety of paintings, sculptures, blown-glass pieces, jewelry, and clay, wood, and paper pieces. Judith Roberts, who taught art in the local public school and is the owner, won national notice a few years back when she worked with a group of handicapped students, whose ages ranged from preschool to twenty-one years, on a huge 10-by-12-foot mural of animals and shrubs. Not only did it win the state competition, but it was eventually displayed at the Kennedy Center in Washington.

Judith says, "I'm really not a terrific salesperson but I get excited talking about art, and I feel that most people like to talk about the paintings that interest them. They like to know something about the artist and why they respond favorably to his or her work. That's what I talk to them about—why a piece appeals to them, and I use basic compositional values in explaining its interest. Sometimes at midnight, I'll have twelve people in here. I've sold a painting at 1:00 in the morning." Hours are 10:00 A.M. to 6:00 P.M. Monday through Saturday. Closed Sunday.

The **Blue Cactus** restaurant in Five Points is definitely a must. Located at 2002H Greene Street, Columbia 29205, the restaurant's decor is eclectic, with a sombrero hanging from the ceiling, a bookcase of hot sauces, postcards from customers from around the world, a world map with pins to show where customers are from, and a little display of snuff cans (very funky)—and this is just the beginning. Recommended lunch fare would be the Be Bim Bop (basically a bowl of rice with an assortment of Korean-style vegetables on top), a choice of beef, chicken, or tofu, and usually an egg served on top of that—you break the egg on top and mix it all up. (Request what you want or don't want on it!) For dinner, try the Curry Chicken Stir Fry (the owner's own recipe). Dinner for two, with appetizers and drinks, will cost under $20. And don't forget the tasty appetizers: Kim Bob (Korean Seaweed Roll—all vegetable) or Korean Dumplings (meat, cabbage, clear noodles). You can always top off your meal with a bowl of Japanese Adzuki Ice Cream, Green Tea, or Ginger Ice Cream. The Blue Cactus is truly a family-run place: Lloyd and Mary Reese are the owners and chefs; Mary's sisters and sisters-in-law help out in the back, and a slew of cousins and children help run the place as well. Go early, because they tend to get packed (the food is excellent!), and, as Lloyd's daughter laughingly says, "We're horribly slow, but Dad would say 'arrogantly' slow!" On a scale of five stars or spoons or forks, or whatever, the Blue Cactus would surely get ten of everything!

I guess at some point I have to pick what I think is the best of the best restaurants in the old town. It's not quite "Off the Beaten Path"; as a matter of fact, it's right smack in the middle of Five Points. It's called **Saluda's,** named for the river that runs through the town. The address is 751 Saluda Avenue, Columbia 29205; (803) 799–9500. First of all you have to climb twenty steps to get to it. But every single step is worth it because this has to be the best food and the best service in town. Second, it has the best view of Five Points and the 20-foot fountain that is its centerpiece. Third, in the spring, summer, and fall, Saluda's helps sponsor a Wednesday evening of music with big local and touring bands playing everything: jazz, rock, light rock, bluegrass, and Broadway show tunes. Anyhow, when you're dining at Saluda's, out on the beautiful terrace, you have the best seat in the house for the music because you are literally looking down on it only 30 or 40 feet away.

Along with their extensive wine list of over 250 selections, the chef here offers an eclectic mix of American and Continental cuisine. One of the specials is the huge lamb shank with a veal-basil demi-glaze. Another is the fresh halibut encrusted with freshly grated horseradish. Both are served with rosemary buttermilk mashed potatoes, spinach, asparagus, and grilled tomatoes. Saluda's is open seven days a week—but only from 11:00 A.M. to 3:00 P.M. on Sundays for a spectacular lunch for $9.95. Monday through Saturday the hours are 5:30 to 11:00 P.M. Prices for dinners average around $33.

A good tip would be to show up here some evening for a cool cocktail out on the patio overlooking the fountain. And while you are here, find out what days the orchestra is playing and then make your reservations.

You'll find **Claussen's Inn** at 2003 Greene Street, Columbia 29205 a unique, comfortable, and very attractive place to stay. The old brick building used to be a bakery, and you can still see the logo in the bricks at the front. Inside, the twenty-nine rooms have 20-foot ceilings, and the loft suites have winding staircases. In 1995, when William Styron, Joe Heller, William Manchester, Paul Fussel, James Dickey, Mickey Spillane, and Al Wertheim were in Columbia for a conference, they all stayed here. Rates are from $110 to $140 with a Continental breakfast and refreshments in the afternoon. Claussen's is four blocks from the University and a hundred yards from the center of Five Points. Call (803) 765–0440.

Down the hill about 100 yards from Claussen's is **Garibaldi's,** 2013 Greene Street, Columbia 29205. This is a first-class restaurant with an excellent wine list, a menu that changes daily, superb food, and a very fine staff. My favorite dish is the apricot-smothered, baked-to-a-crisp flounder. The bar is comfortable for long waits, and you have a fine view of Five Points. Prices for dinner range from $12 to $30. Open for dinner only from Sunday through Thursday from 5:30 to 10:30 P.M. and on Friday and Saturday from 5:30 to 11:00 P.M. Call (803) 771–8888.

Across the street and a little farther down the hill is **Yesterday's Restaurant and Tavern,** 2030 Devine Street, Columbia 29205. Out front up on the roof is a cowboy sitting in a bathtub, which is an indicator of the inside atmosphere. Two televisions serve the bar and the local sports fans and university students. The rest of the space has booths and tables, and during lunch they're packed. Here's an idea for you. Skip a couple meals and come here and order the Confederate Fried Steak. It's served with white gravy, any three vegetables you can name, and all the corn bread you can handle. It will not only stick to every rib you've ever had, but it's as close to delicious as anything you'll ever eat. Open Sunday through Tuesday from 11:30 A.M. to 1:00 A.M.; Wednesday through Saturday from 11:30 A.M. to 2:00 A.M.

Yesterday's Restaurant and Tavern

Leaving Yesterday's by the side door, you are directly in front of **Goatfeathers,** an excellent coffeehouse that serves a lot more than just coffee. You can get a whole meal here of soup and French bread, fresh bagels, or fresh croissants. You can get almost any dessert ever created. Goatfeathers is unquestionably one of the best and liveliest bars in town. A round table in the middle of the room seats ten and is loaded with magazines and newspapers. While you're waiting for a table you can flip through the reading material or go next door to the unique **Intermezzo Book Store,** which is owned by Goatfeathers. Browse through their selection of newspapers and magazines from France, Italy, Germany, Israel, and other countries—more than twenty international papers. Recently they've installed a cigar bar with at least forty varieties from all over the world. They also have a good supply of Batman Zippo lighters.

Someone once said that the South knows as much about cooking veal as a hog knows about the Lord's plan for salvation. I shall now lay that myth to rest. At **Dianne's,** 2400 Devine Street, Columbia 29205, just up the hill from Five Points, they make a veal picatta that rivals anything in the five boroughs of New York. The very thin milk-fed veal is sautéed in a light egg batter with fresh herbs and finished with white wine, lemon, and capers. It is a joy and a wonder. The other veals crossing the finish line with colors flying here are: parmigiana, marsala, saltimbocca, Antoinette, and Fellini. The caesar salad here is first rate, as is every one of the appetizers. A good suggestion is to have two appetizers, a salad, and a good bottle of wine. They also have patio dining, but don't try it in July.

On Wednesday night the popular Ross Holmes and his band play Beach Music, show tunes, and standards and will play anything you can name. He does a great job of singing "Summer Wind" and almost anything Sinatra ever recorded. The prices here range from $6.00 for a small pizza to $40.00 for dinner. Great bar here, with interesting bartenders and a good supply of local characters. Try it, you can't go wrong. Hours for dining are Sunday through Thursday 5:00 to 10:00 P.M., Friday and Saturday 5:00 to 11:00 P.M. Call (803) 254–3535.

Here's something you simply have to try, the *Grazin Monkey* for crab cakes and cold beer. This has to be the best in the Carolinas and you can get it served all by itself. As a matter of fact, after one cake, you'll probably go for two. I did. The rest of the menu is as good and the wide variety should please any jaded taste.

Now appearing behind the bar, direct from Las Vegas, is Columbia's own Eddie Early. Tell him you know me personally and he'll give you four quarters for a dollar, or ten dimes, if you prefer.

The Grazin Monkey is located at 2406 Devine Street, Columbia 29205. Call (803) 256–1072. the bar is open from 4:00 P.M. to midnight; dinner hours are from 5:30 to 11:00 P.M. Closed Sundays.

On a budget and you've got to have chicken? At *Birds on a Wire,* 2631 Devine Street, Columbia 29205, you can't beat the price and the quality. For $6.95 you get half a chicken with two sides and a dinner roll. "Birds" has a nice wine list and an excellent pork tenderloin over cheese grits. Crawfish tails are $9.75; also on the menu are tuna steak and Thai Shrimp and grits. There's a relaxed and easygoing atmosphere here with high-IQ waitresses courtesy of University of South Carolina just down the road. Lunch 11:30 A.M. to 2:30 P.M., dinner from 5:00 to 10:00 P.M., closed Sundays.

Okay, tell me this. Where in all South Carolina, and maybe North Carolina and most of Georgia, can you find Candy Cigarettes, Mary Janes, Bazooka Pops, B.B. Bats, a twenty-five cent cigarette machine, an eight-ounce Coke machine, and a metal sign advertising Hambone Cigars for only five cents? Answer: *The Filling Station.*

This is an old Texaco Station at 2901 Devine Street, Columbia 29205, beautifully converted into a terrific spot for soup, sandwiches, and salad lunches and dinners. They also do a thriving take-out business and cater to small crowds or large.

Specialties include two soups daily, assorted salads, and a wide variety

The Filling Station

of great sandwiches. For you northern transplants they stock Asby's Famous Ice Cream, Boar's Head meats and cheeses, and Dr. Brown's Cream Soda and Beer. Along with all this they have an amazing wine list, with prices ranging from $1.25 per glass to a $200 bottle of Dom's, if you're really in trouble back at the motel.

Inside, the walls are hung with hub caps, a rear bumper from a '57 Chevy Bel-Air (back when they didn't spare the chrome), and a wide assortment of muffler parts and fan belts. You can dine here under the hubcaps or outside under the umbrellas, in between the pumps—Trust the Man behind the Star, Go Texaco—and watch the world go gliding by as you try to figure out the local accents.

Hours are 11:00 A.M. to 7:00 P.M. Monday–Friday, 11:00 A.M. to 5:00 P.M. Saturday; closed Sunday. Call (803) 254–6469.

A recent addition to Five Points is the ***three stage fountain,*** landscaped with beautiful flowering annuals and stone benches, where you can have your morning coffee and muffin from any one of the three or four very good coffeehouses nearby or a Smoothie from right across the street at ***Planet Smoothie.*** The best view of the fountain is from the seats facing south, west, or east—from the north you will have to close your eyes to escape a never-ending series of Exxon signs (at last count there were sixteen).

Nestled directly behind the Adam's Mark Hotel in the heart of the heart of Columbia, at 1230 Hampton Street, where it has been for ten years, is Columbia's premier lunchtime spot: ***The Hampton Place Cafe.*** Not fancy but great! Specializing in gourmet sandwiches, homemade crab and spinach-mushroom quiches, and Greek and Caesar Salads, owner Steve Gendel packs them in every day for lunch. The average price with drink is around $6.00. His only advice is that you get there early to get a seat.

Hampton Place is a great spot to use as a center for seeing the new downtown Columbia. One block away is the brand new and wonderfully set up Columbia Museum of Art, which houses a truly fabulous permanent collection.

Across the street from the museum is *Rising High,* which has two locations in Columbia (see page 134). This is a marvelous renovation of the art-deco Kress Dime Store Building from the 1930s. Almost all the artifacts and decorations have been preserved, as well as the entire front façade, which is covered with gold leaf. It's a masterpiece of renovation and a brilliant landmark in Columbia's new downtown recovery. From Rising High, you can stroll three blocks down Main to the State House and the surrounding parks.

Hampton Place is open from 11:00 A.M. to 3:00 P.M. Monday through Friday. Call (803) 254–5847.

About a mile south of the capitol, the *Rosewood Market and Deli,* at 2803 Rosewood Drive, Columbia 29205, is a one-of-a-kind success story for natural and organic foods. The Deli operates six days a week and features hot meals twice daily. Much of the food here has a macrobiotic slant, but some dairy and fish are occasionally used. Cooking classes are held in the kitchen here on Sundays. On any given day you can find local and international artists happily spooning up their tofu on the outside patio. Call (803) 765–1083.

Doghouse Diner at 800 Harden Street, Columbia 29204 (803–254–9999), is open from 8:00 A.M. to 2:00 A.M. This is a great place to keep in mind for almost any kind of fast food served at almost any hour. The restaurant also has a pool table, video games, a comfortable bar, outdoor seating right in the heart of Five Points, and a lively crowd of steady customers. You can sit outside, eat, listen to the juke box music and watch the 20-odd-foot fountain lighting up the night. *USA Today* and PBS rated it as one of the Top Ten Doghouses in the Country. Don't miss it.

If you're really hungry, visit *Gilligan's Barbecue and Seafood* at 2006 Senate Street, Columbia 29205, which is perhaps my favorite spot for sheer color, food, and activity. Behind the ragtag bar is an autographed eight-by-ten of Bob Denver from *Gilligan's Island*—he's visited here and approves of everything Tim Petersen, the owner, has done to duplicate the old sitcom feeling. The building, which looks as if it's been slung together with driftwood and sheet iron signs, fits snugly up under a truly wonderful magnolia tree, and flowing out in all directions we find the following: a full-scale sand volleyball court, a croquet court, a bocce court, a ping-pong table, horseshoes, and enough room out on the grass for outdoor dining for a couple hundred. Inside there are darts, a full-sized pool table, and enough memorabilia to keep anyone gawking.

Tim also prides himself on his seafood dishes and his barbecue, all at reasonable prices ranging from $6.00 to $9.00. And if you would like a sermon on barbecue, this is the spot to stop because Tim is the man to listen to. He prides himself on serving only barbecue from what in the trade is called "three down ribs," which translates into only small, expensive hogs of less than 110 pounds, which in turn means less fat. He actually closes his eyes and shudders when he mentions barbecue buffets where you can eat all you want. "Man, all that fat will kill you quicker than a train." He says the longer, bigger ribs served in those places are from hogs weighing considerably more than 110, more like 400 and up, with two and three times the amount of fat. But there's more to barbecue than just high-low fat percentages. What you'll want to do is have a beer here with him and find out about barbecue sauces and seafood and how he makes his delicious cole slaw and hush puppies. A place you'll not want to miss. Needless to say, dress is casual. Call (803) 252–5252.

One of the most enjoyable things I did while researching this book was walk in the ***Francis Beidler Forest*** in Four Holes Swamp in Harleyville. To get there from Columbia, take I–26 south to exit 187 and follow the signs to the forest. A 1 1/2-mile boardwalk takes you through the largest remaining virgin stand of bald cypress and tupelo gum trees in the world. It is truly awesome. Many of these forest giants rising out of the clear pools and blackwater streams are 1,000 years old, or older, and reach up well over 200 feet. Alligators, snakes, and every conceivable native animal can be seen if you are quiet and stand still. In the evenings you can even see owls and an occasional otter. A self-guiding tour booklet leads you through this natural cathedral in the forest. It's a walk you will never ever forget.

The forest is named for the lumberman-conservationist Francis Beidler, who preserved the area from logging. Unconventional for a lumberman of his time, he allowed much of his timber to stand while taxes, interest, hurricanes, and insects took their toll. After his death in 1924 his family and later the National Audubon Society and the Nature Conservancy raised the money to continue his program and even expand the sanctuary. Today it covers almost 6,000 spectacular acres. If I had one place to visit in South Carolina and only one, I'd go here. Open to the public from 9:00 A.M. to 5:00 P.M. Tuesday through Sunday. Closed Monday, Thanksgiving, December 24, 25, and 31, and January 1. Admission for adults is $5.00; children six to eighteen pay $2.50; children under six are admitted free, as are Audubon Life Members. Call (803) 462–2150 or write Sanctuary Manager, Francis Beidler Forest, 336 Sanctuary Road, Harleyville 29448.

And finally, the most enjoyable thing I did while working on this book was having Tuesday night breakfast at *The Capitol Restaurant* in Columbia in the winter when the legislature was in session. If you start with your back facing the statue of the Confederate soldier in front of the steps of the capitol and walk up Main Street for half a block you'll see the old and fading green awning of the Capitol Restaurant (803–765–0176). It's usually open for breakfast and lunch from 7:00 A.M. to 3:00 P.M. Monday through Saturday, closed Sunday. The Capitol features breakfasts of sausage, eggs, and grits served all day long; you can also get steaks and chops. Everything is good and everything is served speedily and is modestly priced. A steak with all the trimmings crosses the finish line at about $9.00.

If there is such a place as the exact center of Columbia, and maybe even all of South Carolina, where the wires, the politics, and the liaisons all come together, this is it, and it's been this way for the past fifty or so years. It all happens on Tuesday night while the legislature is in session—from the second Tuesday in January to the end of the first week in June. The house band on these Tuesdays includes Commissioner Rudolph Mitchell on keyboard, Comissioner Cecil Bowers on fiddle, and commission employees Oscar Coates and Roy Gainey playing guitars and harmonizing on the songs. The music ranges far and wide from Jimmy Rodgers's blue yodels to Merle Haggard, from Baptist hymns to "Danny Boy" and anything country-modern that's in the air. Local and not-so-local talent show up and take the mike, and once in a while they'll even sing their favorite song. Kurt Vonnegut once croaked out "Red River Valley," and over the years John Irving, Tom Wolfe, Pat Conroy, Garrison Keillor, James Dickey, Nora Ephron, Pauline Kael, Stephen Spender, John Gardner, and Bruce Springsteen have all taken the mike and said, "Hello, I'm sure glad to be here."

The high point of the Tuesday nights here is the wild and woolly rendition of "Orange Blossom Special," with Cecil smoking on his fiddle and

The Capitol Restaurant, Columbia

congressmen and the local citizens heel-and-toe clogging in the aisles, yipping out enough yeeeee-haaaaws to keep the beer glasses rattling. After the reverberations die down—it takes a while—a hush comes over the room as Oscar Coates chords his guitar and lets the sound hang in the air. Then he'll lean in on the microphone: "OK. Now remember. No dancing during gospel." And he'll segue into "I'll Fly Away," singing with an intensity of feeling that brings tears to the eyes of the faithful and is absolutely beyond description.

There will be a PRIVATE PARTY sign on the door; ignore it and come on in and ask for John. Or hell, ask for me.

At 116 State Street, West Columbia 29169, you can find a row of restaurants, including the very quaint and very cool *Courtyard,* owned by Jay Shreve (a wonderful, animated storyteller in his own right). It has outdoor seating and the atmosphere is straight comfort. On any given day you will find high school students mixed with college students mixed with business executives, all talking to each other and enjoying the wide range of espressos and delicious food.

While you're there, you may want to have one of Jay's Specials, which would consist of any number of different sandwiches and includes pasta and a very fresh fruit salad (a real seller!). He also has a most unique espresso menu, with the leading sellers being the Almond Jay (a mochaccino steamed with almond syrup and topped with whipped cream) and the Milky Way (a mochaccino steamed with caramel syrup and topped with whipped cream). On a hot day, be sure to ask for an Iced Milky Way!

South Carolina State Fair Late October

*P*art of the joy of living down here in the "Hard Lard Belt" and celebrating surviving the summers is fall and the **South Carolina State Fair** in late October. It's the biggest extravaganza down here. There is nothing even close to it. For exact days, call the Columbia Chamber of Commerce at (803) 733–1110. A few of the contests are biscuit making from scratch, Rebel yells, clogging, chicken imperson-ations, hog steeple-chases and duck slides. And through it all are more lights, neon, and calliope and country music than the average person can stand. One wag calls the country music "ignorance set to music." If you decide to go, take my advice, lose a few pounds before you set foot on the premises because every red-blooded church in town has a food booth and everything is knock-down delicious.

Last year, for no apparent reason, I drifted over to the Hog Show and asked a few questions that I'd been saving up for a few years. The big one was how the judges pick a champion hog. The judge I cornered told me more than I wanted to know; this man had all the facts. "Friend, we judge hogs on one point and one point only: how much meat that fellow can

deliver. If there's one extra pork chop on that hog, I don't care if he's got one eye and four ears, that hog is our num-ber one. Friend, raising hogs is a busi-ness, this ain't no kennel club." He kept calling me friend. "Friend, you got to figure the less overall fat, the more hog you'll get for your money. Now take a fat, wide fellow with a lot of extra jowl hanging down. That hog ain't good for nothing. And I mean nothing, in my estimation, turns a judge off faster than a hog that can't walk."

I asked him why, if everything was so slide-ruled out for the butcher counter, the owners hot-combed and powdered the hogs before showing. "Well friend, it's the exact same reason a girl will primp in front of a mirror. Showman-ship! They want that hog to step out there with the best possible chance." He handed me a tract and a bumper sticker, "HOGS ARE BEAUTIFUL." "We're out to improve the image of the hog and maybe bring a little of that beef money down to us. Lot of people figure hogs are dirty and will eat any-thing you put in front of them. Friend, you give a hog a chance and he'll live a lot cleaner than most people." So much for hogs.

Food is served until midnight, and get this, the most you'll pay for a reg-ular meal with tea is $5.75. Not bad! And if you're lucky enough to get there on Thursday nights, you'll hear live acoustic music (and you might even catch the up-and-coming Columbia star, Ray Thom!). Hours are 11:30 A.M. to midnight, Monday through Saturday and noon to midnight on Sunday. Call (803) 791–5663.

On the same street, at 100 State Street, West Columbia 29169, is **Mangia Mangia,** a very upscale, uptown restaurant. Reservations are required, and they have valet parking! The menu is quite extensive and will run you anywhere from $7.00 to $8.00—if you order one of the delicious and filling appetizers—to around $22.00 for an entree with wine. You won't want to miss their Osso Bucco, a traditional Italian dish made up of a roasted lamb shank, Tuscan beans, potatoes, carrots, and onions. You'll feel as if you are in another city eating here; it is dark and romantic, yet cosmopolitan and usually very crowded, and always fun. This is an exciting restaurant owned by Paul Chernoff, and often you will find his sister, Jessie, handing out menus and a million-buck smile! Open Monday through Thursday, 5:00 to 10:00 P.M., and Friday and Saturday from 5:00 to 11:00 P.M. (However, the fabulous bar is open until the last customer leaves—always a good sign!) Closed on Sunday. Call (803) 791–3443.

One more barbecue stop, but this one is different. It's only open on Fridays and Saturdays. Owned and operated by Gerald and Carol Meyer, with Carol's sister Diane helping out, **Meyers Barbecue House** is one of the fastest growing restaurants in this part of the state. The place is small and if you miss the Blythewood cutoff, 18 miles north of Columbia on I–77, it's very hard to find. If you do miss it ask anyone you see. Everyone knows about it. On the other hand, if you make the cutoff when you're supposed to and go 500 yards to the right, there it is on the right.

Once inside the clean, well-lighted but small establishment, you have a choice of barbecued pork or chicken with sides of potato salad, corn, yams, slaw, green beans, and baked beans. And that is it. But that is enough. In the event you can't decide what barbecue and what sauce you want, they will serve you a free sample. Everything here is first rate, cooked on the premises, and the prices are easygoing. A barbecue sandwich is $3.25; chicken, $3.00. Sides are extra but with a soft drink and a side, you can get out of there for less than $6.00. If you decide to eat here, which I did, extra sauce of your choice is served in a squeeze bottle. Excellent for take-out and large catered affairs. Call (803) 754–7400.

While doing this book, I've used the word *best* only a couple of times. Well, here's one more, but this one would be a mortal sin to leave out— the best breads and muffins in all of South Carolina. *Rising High* at 827 Harden Street in Five Points, a hundred yards from the fountain, has its own bakery and specializes in using only fresh and natural ingredients. My advice is to come before 11:30 A.M. or after 2:00 P.M. because the lunch rushes here are fierce. My favorite muffin here is the cranberry, where there is just enough muffin to hold the cranberries together. Owned and operated by two enterprising locals, Kirkman Finlay and

Brian Owen, this is an ideal spot to stop for breakfast, lunch, or to pick up a loaf of bread or a great box lunch for the road. Call (803) 254–3113.

To reach *Lexington Arms,* from downtown Columbia take Highway 1, 14 miles north to 316 West Main Street, Lexington 29072. Around here Highway 1 is called the Two Notch Road, until it gets out of town. Then it changes to U.S. 1 and goes on about its business as it runs on up the road to Maine. It begins at the first phone pole in Florida down at Key West. Anyway, this is the home of Elizabeth and Duncan Crowe and their five children, and probably the best and most varied menu in the Carolinas and Georgia.

At fifteen, in the famous Swiss Hotel school, La Ron, Elizabeth was one of the few women enrolled, but while the others wanted to be dietitians, she began her career as a chef. Today, she says, despite the hard work and long hours, some of her happiest moments were at La Ron, where she learned the fine art of German and French cuisine. "I still remember those chefs dressed in white with their silver spoons around their necks." When she finished school, she had planned to return to her home in Heidelburg to help her mother open a cafe, but being independent, she followed a different course. "I ran away. My mother always had big plans of opening a hotel and dining club. She was going to be the boss and I was going to do all the work. In Europe, women in the kitchen were usually paid lower wages and often forced to give away their cooking secrets. With my papers from La Ron, I knew I could always get work in America, or, for that matter, anywhere."

Elizabeth's husband Duncan, whom she met in Kansas City, where she was manager of the Riverboat Restaurant, was born in London and began his career in the wine trade, working as a wine salesman. He went to the West Indies in the hotel business, then transferred to Kansas City, where he met Elizabeth. After their marriage, they operated a resort hotel in Antigua, and lived and worked in Florida before coming to Lexington and purchasing the Lexington Arms.

Elizabeth says she and Duncan have "some sort of aversion to big cities that developed when we lived on the island. It was small. Everybody knew everybody. That's why we are so happy here in Lexington." Duncan added that they wanted to establish the same kind of familiar atmosphere at the Lexington Arms. "We want it to develop into a community area, a cafe setting. We want people to feel it's their restaurant, whether they want a full meal or just a cup of coffee or a glass of beer. As a matter of fact, if you sit at the bar and decide to have a full meal there, that's fine with us."

Lexington Arms

From the outside, the Lexington Arms looks like a British pub. But Elizabeth and Duncan have taken great care to brighten up the interior and have made it casual and comfortable and a great place just to come in for a beer. The combination of Elizabeth's German, French, and Swiss cuisine and Duncan's British background has resulted in exactly what they wanted—a first-class restaurant that specializes in German, French, and Swiss cuisine, with, of course, many standard American entrees and Caribbean, as well as a very fine and complete wine list.

The wine bar allows you to order some of the finest wines by the glass—the perfect way to try something new.

Elizabeth and Duncan's sons, Charles and Phillip, both now chefs, help out in the kitchen, so the Crowe dynasty is in very good shape for many, many years to come.

Hours are 5:30 P.M. to midnight Monday–Saturday. Closed Sundays. German dishes are served only on Monday, Thursday, and Saturday, and French dishes only on Tuesday and Wednesday. The lounge opens at 4:00 P.M. Call (803) 359–2700.

Richard Riley, formerly governor of South Carolina and now Secretary of Education, once waved his arms and pronounced that Rhoten's sausage featured at **Rhoten's General Store** at 720 Main Street, Lexington 29072, was the best of the best in the Palmetto State. Since that time there have been a few small changes: First, Rhoten's General Store went out of business; second, it is now in the mattress business. Today the old store is stacked to the ceiling and window levels with full-, queen- and king-sized mattresses. But the old ways die hard around here and the populace insisted that they continue selling pork sausage, which they are doing. The result is the only store in the Western world that sells mattresses and pork sausage, and *only* mattresses and pork sausage. Secretary Riley never endorsed the mattresses but the folks around here feel sure he would if asked. They all say the mattresses are good, not quite as good as the sausage, but pretty close. So when you come through Lexington, come on in. There's a good chance you won't be in the market for a mattress, but if you get here in the cool months, you can load up on pork sausage. And later you can drop Secretary Richard Riley a card and thank him for his recommendation. Write Richard E. Riley, Secretary of Education, Washington, D.C. Hours at Rhoten's are 8:00 A.M. to 5:00 P.M. Monday through Saturday. Call (803) 359–6219

Directly across Main Street from Rhoten's General Store you can't miss the sprawling **Lexington Old Mill,** which is indeed an old mill converted to two restaurants and a half-dozen shops specializing in garden gifts, antiques, Old Mill baskets, and fine art and custom framing. Inside are two restaurants, **Mr. Friendly's New Southern Cafe** and **Mungoni's Pizza.**

Mr. Friendly serves up good, old-fashioned New Southern cuisine in a casually sophisticated atmosphere. If you have children, the waiter will give them bowls of bread crumbs to feed the fish in the mill pond that comes right up to the restaurant. No danger here. Mr. Friendly's is open Monday through Saturday, 5:00–10:00 P.M., closed Sunday. Call (803) 359–2999.

Mungoni's advertises being the closest thing to New York–style pizza you'll find—unless you're in New Jersey. Call (803) 951–3550. Mungoni's Pizza is open Monday through Thursday 11:00 A.M. to 9:30 P.M., Friday and Saturday 11:00 A.M. to 10:30 P.M., and Sundays 4:00–9:00 P.M.

The Patchwork Playhouse, a very popular and excellent theater company, also makes it's home here.

Inside the **Flight Deck Restaurant** in downtown Lexington at 109A Old Chapin Road, there is something you simply cannot leave South Carolina without seeing—a 15-foot-plastic cast of mighty King Kong straddling the Empire State Building. With his right hand he is holding on to the antenna on top of the building and glowering at the attacking planes that will eventually be his undoing, while with his left he is crushing a 6-foot model of a Stearman bi-plane. Your kids will be talk-

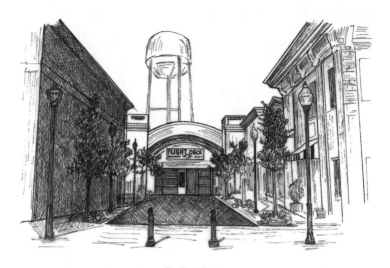

The Flight Deck

ing about this forever. Meanwhile, if there is any red blood in your system, you will be absolutely awestruck by the collection of incredible model planes that cover the ceiling, the foyers, and every inch of wall space. Now I'm not talking about hand-held models you wind up with rubber bands and fly across a room or down a hallway. I'm talking about a P-47 Thunderbolt with a 12-foot wingspan, an enormous P-51, huge B-17's, 24's, 29's, and modern jet fighters. The range is incredible and only a madman or someone like Ted Stambolitis, who owns and operates the place, would have dared do all this by himself. Yes, he built the planes, hung them, and knows every inch of each of them. And he will be delighted to show you around and answer any and all questions. Incidentally, Ted, also a licensed pilot, has actually flown everything from hang gliders to experimental aircraft.

But more than just a museum of old planes, the Flight Deck is a busy, very successful restaurant specializing in sandwiches, buffet meals, and desserts, including old-fashioned milk shakes and malted made and served in old-time shake cans if you like them that way. Everything here is first rate, moderately priced, and exceptionally clean. It's an ideal place to bring, and maybe even leave, the kids.

Hours are Monday-Thursday 11:00 A.M. to 9:30 P.M. Friday–Saturday 11:00 A.M. to 11:00 P.M. Closed Sundays. Call (803) 957–5990.

PLACES TO STAY IN UPLANDS AND COLUMBIA

COLUMBIA
Chestnut Cottage B&B
1718 Hampton
Columbia 29201
(803) 256–1718

Rose Hall B&B
1006 Barnwell
Columbia 29201
(803) 771–2288

EDGEFIELD
Cedar Grove Plantation
1365 Highway 25 North
Edgefield 29824
(803) 637–3056

GREENVILLE
Creekside Plantation
3118 South Highway 14
Greenville 29356
(864) 297–3293

Pettigru Place B&B
302 Pettigru Street
Greenville 29601
(864) 242–4529

LANDRUM
Country Mouse Inn
120 North Trade Avenue
Landrum 29356
(864) 457–4061

Red Horse Inn
310 North Campbell Road
Landrum 29356
(864) 895–4968

ROCK HILL
Book & Spindle
626 Oakland Avenue
Rock Hill 29730
(803) 328–1913

East Main Guest House
600 East Main
Rock Hill 29730
(803) 366–1161

SALEM
Sunrise Farm B&B
325 Sunrise Drive
Salem 29676
(864) 944–0121

SPARTANBURG
Nicholls-Crook
Plantation B&B
120 Planation Drive
Woodruff 29388
(864) 476–8820

Walnut Lane B&B
110 Ridge Road
Lyman 29365
(864) 949–7230

UNION
Inn at Merridun
100 Merridun Place
Union 29379
(864) 427–7052

Juxa Plantation
117 Wilson Road
Union 29379
(864) 427–8688

PLACES TO EAT IN UPLANDS AND COLUMBIA

BUFFALO
Midway Barbecue
811 Hash Boulevard
Buffalo 29321
(869) 427–4047

COLUMBIA
Dianne's on Devine
2400 Devine Street
Columbia 29205
(803) 254–3535

Garibaldi's
2013 Greene Street
Columbia 29205
(803) 771–8888

Goatfeathers Coffee Bar &
Restaurant
2017 Devine Street
Columbia 29205
(803)256–3325

Longhorn Steakhouse
902 Gervais Street
Suite A
Columbia 29201
(803) 254–5100

Motor Supply Company
920 Gervais Street
Columbia 29201
(803) 256–6687

Za's Brick Oven Pizza
2930 Devine Street
Columbia 29205
(803) 771–7334

GREENVILLE
Cafe & Then Some
101 College Street
Greenville 29601
(864) 232–2287

SPARTANBURG
Gerhard's Cafe
1200 East Main Street
Spartanburg 29307
(864) 591–1920

WEST COLUMBIA
Mangia Mangia
100 State Street
West Columbia 29169
(803) 791–3443

General Index

Entries for Museums and Plantations appear in the special indexes on page 146.

INDEX

INDEX

INDEX

Museums

Plantations

About the Author

William Price Fox grew up in the Low Country of South Carolina. He has worked as a salesman in New York, a scriptwriter in Hollywood, and a professor at the Writer's Workshop at the University of Iowa. He is the author of seven novels and short story collections, including *Southern Fried Plus Six, Ruby Red,* and *Chitlin Strut & Other Madrigals.* His articles and short stories have been published in magazines and newspapers such as *Sports Illustrated, Travel & Leisure, Golf Digest, Esquire, The Saturday Evening Post,* and the *Los Angeles Times.* He currently is the producer and moderator of the University of South Carolina E.T.V. Writer's Workshop Program and lives in Columbia.